THE LOVE ONE ANO

LEADER'S GUIDE
LEAD YOUR GROUP TO CLOSER PERSONAL RELATIONSHIPS

A Bible Study by

Churches Alive!

MINISTERING TO THE CHURCHES OF THE WORLD
600 Meridian Avenue, Suite 200
San Jose, California 95126-3427

Published by

NAVPRESS
BRINGING TRUTH TO LIFE
NavPress Publishing Group
P.O. Box 35001, Colorado Springs, Colorado 80935

Second printing, 1994

Cover photographs: Willard Clay

Printed in the United States of America

*Because we share kindred aims for helping local churches fulfill Christ's Great
Commission to "go and make disciples," NavPress and Churches Alive have
joined efforts on certain strategic publishing projects that are intended to bring
effective disciplemaking resources into the service of the local church.*

*For more than a decade, Churches Alive has teamed up with churches of all
denominations to establish vigorous disciplemaking ministries. At the same time,
NavPress has focused on publishing Bible studies, books, and other resources
that have grown out of The Navigators' 50 years of disciplemaking experience.*

*Now, together, we're working to offer special products like this one that are
designed to stimulate a deeper, more fruitful commitment to Christ in the local
gatherings of His Church.*

*The LOVE ONE ANOTHER series was written by Russ Korth, Ron Wormser, Jr., and
Ron Wormser, Sr. of Churches Alive. Many individuals from both Churches
Alive and NavPress contributed greatly in bringing this project to publication.*

Contents

Introduction

This introduction tells you how to understand and use the rest of this guide. This book is for both leaders and teachers of the Love One Another series.

If you are leading a small group studying Love One Another, you will be working with people who are committed to regular attendance and having their lessons prepared. Therefore, you don't have to lecture. You can lead your group in meaningful discussion of the material. This is the most effective way to guide your members to understand and apply these concepts on building better relationships. Their learning is strengthened as they verbalize their answers and participate in the discussion. Also, they learn from each other.

If you are teaching in a classroom setting, such as a Sunday school, you will not necessarily have the same group every week and some may not have their lessons prepared. You will need to do some lecturing. But, even as a teacher, avoid the "I talk—you listen" routine. Involve the class by having them contribute ideas. Use skits, roleplaying, demonstrations, illustrations, and other devices to help people understand the concepts.

KNOW THE ORGANIZATION

Key Concept—There is a Key Concept for every lesson in the study books. Keep this concept in mind as you prepare the lesson. Help your group put it into clear focus as you cover the material.

Goal—A statement of the goal for that particular lesson will also help you keep your discussion on target.

Background information—Most lessons begin with several paragraphs of background. Use this information to introduce the session.

Helps—There are helps for your leading or teaching. They are numbered to correspond to the question numbers in the study booklets.

Use the numbered helps to develop a plan for leading or teaching your group. You may not use all of the ideas presented. Evaluate them according to the needs of your people.

Teaching Idea—At the end of each section is an idea to help you present the major concepts of the lesson to a group. These ideas are primarily designed for a classroom setting. A small group leader may want to use them from time to time to help present an idea. Be careful not to turn the group into a classroom setting.

For example, if you choose to use an idea that calls for displaying a chart in front of the group you may simply draw the illustration on a large piece of paper. When an idea suggests you should divide into groups to discuss a question, you may not need to. A small group of no more than twelve is already an appropriately sized discussion group.

BE CREATIVE

This leader's guide has good ideas, but it is not exhaustive. You should invent additional ideas to help communicate the concepts to your people. As you use launching, guiding, and application questions, you will learn how to formulate other questions in these areas.

Remember, whether you are a leader or a teacher, you cannot cause people to grow spiritually. Only God can do that. Be available to be used by Him.

FORGIVING

God's Forgiveness

KEY CONCEPT: God's forgiveness is complete.
GOAL: To enjoy an unhindered relationship with God by recognizing the
full extent of God's forgiveness.

One of the basic premises of the Bible is that everything begins with God.
Life began with God, love began with God, possessions come from God.
Everything originates with God.

Forgiveness begins with God in two ways. First, God forgives you
through Jesus Christ. Second, God empowers you to forgive others.

God's forgiveness forms the foundation of the *Forgiving* book and
the entire LOVE ONE ANOTHER series. Seeing God's forgiveness allows you
to forgive others, thus tearing down barriers and developing positive relationships.

1,2. Use these questions to help people see the importance of both
knowing God has forgiven us and feeling forgiven by Him.

3. Ask several people to give a single term and definition from their
charts. Do not discuss definitions; use your time to interact on
other questions.

5. "How do you define God's forgiveness?"

"How do you feel about God's forgiveness?"

6. "In addition to the reasons presented in this passage, why is it
important to you personally to understand God's forgiveness?"

7. "Can you think of another way to illustrate God's forgiveness?"

8. There are many acceptable interpretations of this phrase. A common interpretation of "their sins and lawless acts I will remember
no more" is, "I will not consider your sins in dealing with you."

TEACHING IDEAS: Use a tape recorder to record a mock argument with
yelling and name-calling. Play a short portion of this for the group.
Rewind the tape and erase it. Replay the now-blank tape to illustrate
forgiveness.

For question 7, illustrate Psalm 103:12 by bringing a globe to class.
Show that you can't go farther north than the North Pole. Once you pass
it, you begin going south. Neither can you go farther south than the
South Pole. The distance from north to south is 12,500 miles. But the
distance from east to west is infinite.

Why God Forgives

KEY CONCEPT: God's forgiveness is always available.

GOAL: To live in God's forgiveness, light, and fellowship by immediately confessing sins.

3. "When you think of all that Christ paid to give you forgiveness, how does it make you feel about Him? About yourself? About others?"

4. Be careful not to spend too much time on this question.

5. "How do you define 'perfect' in verse 14?"

6. "What is the difference between having a guilty conscience and being aware of guilt?"

7. If nonChristians are in attendance, amplify this question with additional verses.

8. "What is repentance?"

   "Does feeling sorry mean you've repented?"

   Other verses that help answer this question are Romans 10:9-10 and Galatians 2:16.

   "A fifty-year-old woman had a long-term habit that caused severe physical problems. She decided to quit her habit, saying, 'Staying alive is more important to me than continuing this habit.' Did she repent? Why, or why not? Did she repent in the sense of Isaiah 55:6-7?"

9. "What should you do if you know you have sinned but do not feel any remorse for the sin?"

10. "Does God treat you differently for failing to confess a sin than for refusing to confess a sin?"

11. "What are you doing that helps you live in daily fellowship with God?"

TEACHING IDEA: For question 11, use a flashlight to illustrate walking in the light as described in 1 John 1:7-9. Walking in the light enables you to see what you need to confess. If, instead of confessing, you contend there is nothing wrong, the light is turned off, and you are walking in darkness rather than in the light.

Forgiving Others

KEY CONCEPT: Because God has forgiven you, forgive others.
GOAL: To be a forgiving person regardless of the situation.

Forgiving is not natural. When someone does something against you, it is natural to get angry, to become bitter, or to try to get even. Fortunately, God does not treat you like that. He shows His love, mercy, and forgiveness in Christ. Through Him, you escape all of God's anger and vengeance against sin.

Since you receive so much forgiveness from God, He expects you to forgive others, also. But He does not expect you to forgive others in your own power. You are in Christ, and His Spirit is in you. When you walk in the Spirit, you will not react in the natural way; but you will be loving, merciful, and forgiving.

1. "Why do feuds often involve ever-increasing numbers of people?"

   "How can you keep from being involved?"

3. "Besides the main reason to forgive (God has forgiven us), what are other reasons to forgive?" List these reasons on the chalkboard.

4. "It appears that Peter was looking for the minimum requirement. How do people do this today?"

   "What's wrong with looking for the minimum?"

5. "Besides the main point, what other important points about forgiveness does this parable illustrate?"

7. Do not allow a long discussion about the implications of this verse. It may be difficult to understand, but it does show that Jesus expects you to be forgiving.

8. "Do you think some people enjoy being angry? Why, or why not?"

1-8. Summarize by asking, "From your study of this lesson, what reason for forgiving others is most meaningful to you?"

9. The purpose of this question is to help participants apply what they have learned to hypothetical but common-to-life situations. This should prepare them for actual problems they will face. Since each person will choose one of the four situations, there are actually four different lessons. Whether using a discussion or teaching format, it is best to focus on one situation at a time. Divide your allotted time into fourths and strictly adhere to this schedule so you will have

time to cover all four situations. Most groups will have at least one person for whom each situation is similar to real life.

TEACHING IDEA: Prepare for all four situations in question 9. Be ready to give a three-to-five-minute imaginary testimony about each situation, telling what happened, how you felt, what you did, etc. In your first story, play the part of a person who did not forgive and tell what happened. In the second, take the part of a person who was forgiving and, as a result, good relationships developed. In the third, be a forgiving person, but tell how the relationship is still fragmented. In the fourth, tell how you forgave the other person, but still are experiencing inner turmoil, sleepless nights, etc. After each "testimony," ask the group to give ideas on how to do things better, promises from the Bible to claim, and what to do next.

For question 5, ask some people in the group to act out the parts in the parable of the king and his servants. Encourage the actors to dramatize the event by assuming the attitude of the character they play. Add to the list of reasons for question 3 on the chalkboard as appropriate.

Results of Forgiving

KEY CONCEPT: Everyone benefits from forgiveness.
GOAL: To recognize that forgiveness is done for your own sake as well as for an offender's.

The foundation of forgiveness is God's complete forgiveness of us. Being totally purged of our sins, we can have assurance of our relationship with God. His model should lead us to the decision to be forgiving. Seeing the benefits that result when we forgive will then motivate us on a day-by-day basis to practice forgiving constantly.

Failure to see these benefits will often result in the feeling that forgiveness is "letting the other guy off." In fact, the forgiver usually gains more than the person forgiven.

2. "Do you find it difficult to forgive yourself?"

    "What do you think a person who finds self-forgiveness difficult should do?"

3. "What are some other benefits not listed in these verses?"

4. "Which actions that you listed do you like the most?"

5. Warning: Keep the discussion positive. Don't allow the group to talk about unforgiving people.

    "What do you think would happen if those of us *here* practiced Colossians 3:13?"

6. "What are the ultimate goals of church discipline?"

7. "What are the goals of church forgiveness?"

    "Do you think we should forgive only when we see an expression of sorrow?"

8. "A church is similar to a club, fraternity, or sorority, as they are all groups of people working together. How do these organizations exercise discipline and express forgiveness?"

    "How is that like a church? How is it different?"

TEACHING IDEAS: Draw two columns on the chalkboard and write "Discipline" on one side and "Forgiveness" on the other. Ask the group to list acts that require discipline and others that require forgiveness by a church.

Ask a volunteer to stand before the group, while everyone else helps you construct a list of bodily reactions that occur when you do not forgive others (tense muscles, high blood pressure, ulcers, headaches, etc.). As each malady is mentioned, write it on a piece of paper and tape it to the volunteer's body where that problem would occur. Point out that one of the beneficial results of forgiving is the improved physical condition of your body.

Perspective on Injustice

KEY CONCEPT: God can prevent any evil from harming you.
GOAL: To be free of the anxiety that can overwhelm those who do not have the assurance that God controls all things.

The situations studied in lesson 4 show how difficult it can be to forgive. Perhaps the most difficulty you will have in forgiving others is when you suffer a great injustice. Everyone suffers injustices. The greatest injustice in all history was Jesus' death on the cross. Though He was the only completely righteous person, He was crucified mercilessly.

The cross was the greatest injustice of all time, but it was not a tragedy. It was a victory. Through death, Jesus destroyed death. Through the cross, He redeemed sinners. When you suffer injustices, you can view them as tragedies or you can anticipate the victory that God wants to give you through them.

3. "What do these verses imply about a person who is not cooperating with God's purposes?"

4. "How would you compare the worst you've suffered with what Job suffered?"

   "How did your response to the worst you've suffered compare with Job's response?"

5. "Does 'good' here mean 'pleasurable'?"

   "Which things in Hebrews 11:35-38 do you consider good?"

   "Which things worked for good but were not good in themselves?"

6. "Although David said God induced Shimei to curse him, he may not have fully forgiven him. Read more about this story in 2 Samuel 19:18-23 and 1 Kings 2:8,36-46. Do you think David did the right thing in his dealings with Shimei?"

7. Ask each person in the group to name one thing that happened during the day that he or she didn't like. After all have named one thing, ask one person to lead in prayer and give thanks for all these things.

8. To conserve time, do not read all these passages in the group.

   "How are you like Joseph?"

   "Did you have brothers or sisters?"

   "Was there favoritism in the home?"

"How was sibling rivalry demonstrated?"

"Did you have dreams of leadership?"

"Do you still have them?"

"In what ways do you think the injustices helped prepare Joseph for leadership mentally? Emotionally? In personal security? In sensitivity?"

9. "How does the lesson that you learned from Joseph's life help you?"

10. "Which are you most likely to do when you suffer an injustice: fight, run away, get discouraged, plot revenge, or acquiesce?"

"If your reaction isn't right, how do you think Joseph's example will help you in the future?"

TEACHING IDEAS: Bring a newspaper to the meeting and tell the group you want to read part of an editorial that appeared in yesterday's paper. Then read the following, inserting your pastor's name and the name of your church. Make it look like you are reading from the newspaper.

"It is high time we put a stop to these money-hungry hypocrites and expose them as the emotional abusers they are. Men like . . . of . . . church need to be run out of town and replaced by people who really care about others."

Then suggest the group write a letter to the newspaper to correct the perverted image it gave of your pastor. Before the group gets too excited or riled up, tell them the truth—that no such editorial was written. This exercise is to help them understand how David's followers responded to Shimei, as brought out in question 6.

For question 8, tell the story of Joseph in outline form. When you get to a part where he suffered an injustice, ask some from the group to assume the role of those who hurt Joseph—for example, his brothers when they sold him into slavery. Then, you act out Joseph's role and repeatedly ask them, "Why are you doing this to me?" Their answers may be something like, "Because we don't like you," "Because we are jealous," "Because we are insecure." The group's imaginary answers will often give them insight about interpersonal relationships.

Reacting to Injustice

KEY CONCEPT: God expects us to endure injustices patiently.
GOAL: To have peace while patiently enduring injustices.

The ultimate test for a person who believes God is in control is how he or she reacts to unjust suffering. If I am sure God's control is being exercised in my best interest, I can rejoice that I am being perfected. I may not like the process, but I know I'll be better for it.

  1,2. Most people will have little difficulty listing examples for the first four for themselves and much difficulty citing examples for Jesus. This shows how minimally people usually suffer injustices.

    3. "How does your commitment to God help you when you are facing an injustice?"

   3c. "Jesus did not retaliate or threaten. What are some reasons that people retaliate or threaten today?"

    4. "What can you do that will help you apply James 1:2-4 the next time?"

    5. Each person will need to draw a conclusion based on his or her understanding of the Bible.

    6. "Does the passage in 1 Peter mean we should be pacifists?"

     "Do people in general consider those who suffer patiently, foolish or heroic? Why do you think this is so?"

     "Revenge has been a common theme in movies and TV programs. Can you think of any stories of forgiveness and suffering injustice patiently?"

     "What do you think is the best way to use an unjust situation as a testimony to others?"

    7. "What is a typical way you are treated unfairly while driving? At your work? By your spouse?"

TEACHING IDEA: For question 3, prepare a short skit of a courtroom scene. One person is proven "guilty" of doing many good deeds and is punished for them. Discuss the parallels and contrasts of the skit to the teaching of 1 Peter 2:19-25.

Results of an Unforgiving Spirit

KEY CONCEPT: Forgiving others is often the solution to problems of anger, bitterness, clamor, malice, slander, and vengeance.

GOAL: To avoid the wrong attitudes and bad actions that can flow from lack of forgiveness.

When people do not forgive, other problems arise in their lives from a bed of resentment. Ephesians 4:31 identifies six of these sin problems. Because these sins occur so often, people tend to excuse them instead of dealing with them. They rationalize by saying, "It's only natural." This lesson focuses on the insidious nature of these problems and why it is essential to defeat them by forgiving.

This is a long lesson. If you attempt to discuss every question and answer with your group, it will take too much time. Instead, allot ten minutes for each of the six sections; and stick to the schedule. This way you will cover the lesson in one session.

2. Bitterness is like a root that spreads and grows until it affects your entire being. Keep the discussion of this question and all other definition questions brief.

6. Guiding question: "Why does forgiving uproot bitterness?"

7. Anger is associated with foolishness and destruction. Do not look up all the references used in this question. Instead, ask group members to read what they have written in their booklets. First, they can share all of the characteristics of anger they listed. Then, discuss conclusions about these characteristics. In similar fashion, go through the other three columns.

8. Launching question: "Some have suggested that you count to ten to overcome anger. What other suggestions do you have?"

10. Taking vengeance usurps God's position. Ask several people to read their paraphrases exactly as written in their books before opening the floor to discussion.

11. Guiding question: "What is wrong with plotting revenge even when you don't expect to carry out your plan?"

13. Clamor creates an atmosphere of confusion, disorder, and hostility. Guiding question: "What are some situations where you have seen clamor?"

14. Launching question: "How do you feel when you are around a clamorous person?"

15. Slander ruins people and relationships. Launching question: "What are some ways the tongue is like a fire?"

16. Ask people to illustrate ways slander is used today, without using specific instances, which would be gossip.

20. Malice produces hateful actions. Launching question: "Why is forgiveness essential to conquering these malicious thoughts?"

TEACHING IDEA:

▶ Establish the key concept from Ephesians 4:31-32.
▶ Then divide the group into six smaller groups. Ask each group to study one of the six attitudes that result from an unforgiving spirit.
▶ After about fifteen minutes, ask one member from each group to give a short report on the dangers of the problem they studied.
▶ Conclude the session by going through the teaching of Galatians 5:14-25.

FORGIVING 8
Offending Others

KEY CONCEPT: When you have offended another, interrupt your activities to initiate reconciliation.

GOAL: To initiate reconciliation and improve relationships whenever an offense exists.

You offend others when you cause them to stumble by leading them astray, encourage them to do wrong, or become a barrier to their growth and development. Your offense may be by deed or words. It usually is done through unintentional but insensitive acts.

One of the main problems is that you often do not know that you have offended another. You can't correct things until you know if they really are wrong.

1. "What should you do if you are convinced you've done nothing wrong but someone feels you offended him or her?"

2. "Can you think of other important reasons in addition to those given in Matthew 18?"

3. "Are there other consequences you can think of?"

4. "What should you say to someone who gives this excuse?"

5. "What should you do when you think taking an action will offend someone and *not* taking the same action will offend someone else?"

6. "What are some ways people offend children?"

   "What should you do when the child you have offended is your own son or daughter?"

7. "In what ways do you see yourself as being like Peter in this situation?"

9. "What are some practical steps we can take to avoid offending others?"

   "What can you do to increase your sensitivity to others to keep from offending them?"

TEACHING IDEA: Before the session, arrange for two group members to role-play the following situation (you may have to play one of the roles). At lesson's completion, present the situation to the group and commence the reconciliation "drama."

At a recent potluck dinner, Philip walked up to Bob and said, "Boy, those are really nice clothes—almost as nice as what people are wearing this year." When everyone laughed, Philip continued making other jokes ridiculing Bob. Today, Philip read Proverbs 26:18-19 and was convicted about his behavior. Now he is going to Bob to rectify his error.

FORGIVING **9**
Being Offended

KEY CONCEPT: Initiate reconciliation whenever obstacles exist.
GOAL: To use offenses for growth and better relationships by forgiving
the offender from the heart and confronting the offender in humility.

When an offense occurs, you can use it as an opportunity to build better
relationships by following the directives of the Bible. Never just sit back
and hope things will get better.

1. "What type of offenses seem to occur most often in our society?"

2. "Should you consider it an offense when someone does something
   you do not like?"

   "When someone does something you consider improper?"

   "When your feelings are hurt?"

3. If no one *knows* of a specific example, it may indicate a lack of
   applying the instruction of this Scripture passage. Explain how the
   steps might unfold in your church.

4. "One person said, 'I find that sometimes I don't want the person to
   apologize and be nice about things.' Why do you think he feels that
   way?"

5. "The person in Luke 17 kept apologizing, but did not change
   actions. Do you think he was sincere?"

   "Should we expect a sincere apology before we forgive? If so, what
   constitutes a sincere apology?"

6. "What is your reaction to the fact that these were major church
   leaders having this problem?"

   Avoid focusing on who was right and who was wrong; concentrate
   on how the example can help you and your church avoid offenses
   and handle them correctly when they occur.

7. "Why do we tend to shy away from dealing with offenses?"

   "What does this tendency say about our thoughts of others?"

8. "In what other ways can we protect ourselves from being offended?"

TEACHING IDEA: After presenting the concepts in this chapter, illustrate
them with role-playing. Use the situation with Philip and Bob from the
Teaching Idea in lesson 8. This time, ask Bob to initiate the conversation
with Philip, who seems oblivious to the offense.

UNDERSTANDING

Keys to Understanding

KEY CONCEPT: Seeking the Lord is essential to understanding.
GOAL: To seek the Lord on a daily basis and see others through His eyes.

Understanding means approaching things from another's point of view. When looking through the eyes, experience, and values of another, you sense validity in his or her perspective.

Understanding results in acceptance but not always agreement. The understanding person acknowledges the right of others to hold their opinions and express their emotions. The understanding person says, "I can see why you might say that," even while disagreeing. Understanding is not required when there is full agreement. It is understanding that allows and enables people to build relationships despite sharp disagreements.

2. "How important is it for you to feel you are understood by people with whom you desire a close relationship?"

3. "Why does seeking God lead to understanding?"

   "How can we seek the Lord daily?"

4. "Which of the activities that we have mentioned has been the most helpful to you?"

   "How can you strengthen these activities in your life?"

5. "Are you ever jealous of carefree and wealthy people?"

   "Would you agree with the psalmist's conclusion in verses 16-18? Why, or why not?"

   "What other thoughts keep you from jealousy?"

6. "Someone said, 'You can't seek God while pursuing your own thoughts.' Why do you agree or disagree with this statement?"

   "Why will having God's perspective help you understand other people?"

7. "Why do these things increase our understanding?"

8. "What do you think we could accomplish if we were totally united in heart and purpose?"

9. "Are these verses encouraging us to be skeptical and negative? Explain your answer."

11. "Why does this action reflect understanding?" Can be asked after each of the evidences.

13. "We are a part of the church. What can we do in this group to improve our understanding of one another?"

14. "What values do you think Solomon had that caused him to ask for understanding?"

    "Which of the values (discussed by group) are an evidence of already having understanding?"

TEACHING IDEA: Before the group meeting, hide a dollar bill or something else of value in the room. Before you begin the lesson, tell the group what you have hidden and that the person who finds it will get to keep it. Later, when presenting the concept of seeking the Lord, ask what they did to seek for the hidden prize and how that is like seeking the Lord. Then discuss ways in which seeking God is different from seeking the prize.

UNDERSTANDING 2
Empathy

KEY CONCEPT: Experiences with others help you share feelings.
GOAL: To share in the feelings of others.

In lesson 1, understanding others was approached on the mental basis—that is, by seeing through the eyes of God and of the other person. Now, understanding is approached on the emotional level—through empathy.

Empathy differs from sympathy. It means "feeling with" or experiencing the same emotions. It involves identification with another. Sympathy is "feeling for" or being sorry for someone. It does not go to the depth of understanding that empathy does, and sometimes it encourages self-pity, discouragement, and hopelessness.

1. "Why do you think empathy is important in building relationships with others?"

2. "Can you relate a specific experience when you had these feelings and someone expressed empathy?"

4. "How are you helped by knowing that others are tempted in the same way you are?"

    "Why do we have such a hard time admitting we are tempted? After all, we're not admitting that we sinned."

5. "What do you think is the significance of the extremes used in this verse?"

6. "What should we do if we feel Jesus is ashamed of us?"

9b. "How do you *feel* when you consider all Jesus has done to empathize with you?"

10. "What can we do to prepare ourselves to empathize with someone who is vastly different from us—such as a prostitute, a drug dealer, or a murderer?"

TEACHING IDEA: Ask a man and a woman to volunteer to read the two following statements. Use people who can embellish them with a liberal amount of ad libs.

> HE: "I come home from work and I'm tired. I want to sit down for just five minutes, but no sooner do I sit down than she starts nagging me about all the jobs that need to be done around the house. This past week, I must have spent about fifty hours working on things around the house. I get more relaxation at the office than at home. I don't know what it will take to please her."

SHE: "I try never to mention jobs that he has to do. He comes home and turns on the television and then sits and watches two or three football games with nothing more than a grunt toward me. Then, while I'm bringing him another dish of ice cream, if I happen to mention that the garbage needs to be taken out, he blows his top. I'm fed up with it."

Ask the men in the group to offer suggestions on how the man in the skit can empathize with his wife. Likewise, ask the women to make suggestions for the woman.

Recognizing Differences

KEY CONCEPT: Don't be critical of those who are different.
GOAL: To relate to people without qualifiers or expectations.

Differences are the reason we work on understanding. If you agree with my ideas, I think I understand you; you are a clear thinker. If you agree with my feelings, I think I understand you; you have a balanced temperament. If you act like I act, I think I understand you; you are a normal person.

But as you differ from me in these areas, you become strange, unbalanced, and abnormal to me. Understanding removes these barriers to relationships.

1. "What are some differences that create barriers between various people?"

3. "Why do you think it is important to know that these particular differences exist?"

4. "What do you conclude in light of the fact that several people cited in Hebrews 11 experienced adversity?"

6a. "What are some of the ways Jesus and John were similar?"

"Thinking only of the descriptions of these two in this passage, what kind of person today is like Jesus?"

"What kind is like John?"

8. "When do you tend to react like Peter and ask about others instead of focusing on your own responsibility?"

9. "How might people today express the same reactions that the Corinthians had?"

10a. "What are some of the ways this unwise practice is carried out today?"

TEACHING IDEA: Make four columns on the chalkboard, as in the illustration.

DIFFERENCES IN:

GOD'S WORK	EXPERIENCE	LIFESTYLE	OTHER
Gifts	Miracles	Unusual (John)	Temperament
Calling	Deliverance	Associated with common	Looks
Ministry	Good times	people (Jesus)	Likes and dislikes
	Bad times		

FOLLOW JESUS!

In the first column, list differences that are a result of God's work discovered in question 3. In the next column, list different experiences from question 4. In the third column, list different lifestyles, as found in question 6. List the ideas that do not fit any of these categories in the fourth column.

Conclude this session by showing that everyone, regardless of differences, should follow Jesus as brought out in question 8, completing the diagram as in the illustration.

Accepting Differences

KEY CONCEPT: Accept others as they are.
GOAL: To accept others with different ideas, customs, values, and back-grounds without reservation.

Recognizing that there are numerous and sometimes vast differences among us does not guarantee understanding. Even acknowledging that these differences are legitimate won't always help. There must be the understanding that produces acceptance despite the differences.

1. "How did this experience make you feel?"

   "How did this experience affect you later in life?"

3. Ask several people in the group to read their responses, following this pattern: "I usually *show my feelings*. Some think I am *friendly and caring*. Others think I am *flighty and emotional*." Ask them to read their responses to the second and third parts, following the same format.

   "What insight did you get by reading how others might respond to you?"

   "According to the chart, 'friendly' and 'flighty' are two ways people might consider a person who shows feelings. Do you think there are generally both positive and negative ways to consider the same behavior in a person? Explain."

4. "What kind of changes does God want us to make?"

   "There are certainly bad (or sinful) actions, but is there such a thing as a bad personality or temperament? Explain."

5. "As you were growing up, did your parents or friends tell you not to accept a certain group of people? What helped you overcome this ingrained prejudice?"

   "What are some other ways to glorify God?"

   "How can we have the unity described in Romans 15:6, if we wish to use a variety of ways to glorify God?"

7. "What are some ways to express acceptance of a person and still express disapproval for sinful activities?"

8. "What has given you an increased assurance that you will be accepted by others in your church, even if you confess your sins in front of them?"

TEACHING IDEA: Show someone a ten-dollar bill and ask if he or she would like to have it. Then fold it and ask the same question. Fold it again and ask again. Finally, crumple it into a wad and ask one more time. The person would always like to have the bill, because no matter what condition it is in, it is always worth ten dollars. In the same way, you should accept others, no matter what condition they are in, because they are always of value.

Accommodating Others

KEY CONCEPT: Accommodating others can improve relationships and open doors to communicate the gospel.

GOAL: To modify your behavior for the comfort or benefit of others without compromising any moral standard.

In the previous section, you studied differences and the need to accept people who are different from you. Accommodating takes the process one step further. Not only do you accept differences, you modify your behavior to fit the other person.

By saying, "I can see why you are upset," you accommodate another person's attitude and soothe a tense situation. By preparing a pot of coffee for a friend's visit (when you don't like coffee), you accommodate his or her desires and demonstrate understanding.

Accommodating is one of those areas in the Christian life that requires discernment and balance. Too much accommodation can be compromise.

1. "How can you regard others as better than yourself when you know they really aren't better?"

2. "This passage presents Jesus as an example for us. Can you think of a specific instance when He accommodated someone? What were the positive results of His action?"

3. Referring to 1 Corinthians 8:13, a pastor said he would wear a tie to the Bible study (where no one else wore one) to be sure that he would never offend someone. One layman replied, 'But your wearing the tie offends me.' What do you think the pastor should do?"

4,5. "These questions provide a contrast between accommodating and not accommodating people. From these examples, what are some general rules for the correct way to accommodate others?"

Some other questions that can generate discussion: "Does that rule require courage or come from fear?"

"Is it for my ease or another's benefit?"

"Do I fear what others might think, or am I flaunting independence?"

7. The Bible does not tell us whether Paul's action at Lystra was right or wrong. Each person in the group will need to evaluate Paul's action.

"What do you think would have happened if Paul had not circumcised Timothy?"

8. "What is a parallel action that takes place today?"

9. "What is the difference in the intent of the accommodator and the man-pleaser?"

"What is the difference in deeds?"

TEACHING IDEA:

▶ Draw three columns on the chalkboard.
▶ Write "Too Little" at the top of the left-hand column and talk about what happens when you do not accommodate enough. Get ideas from your study and the diagram below.
▶ Then, atop the right-hand column, write "Too Much," and tell what can happen when someone over accommodates.
▶ Finally, develop the middle column, which has the "Correct" amount of accommodating.

ACCOMMODATING

TOO LITTLE	CORRECT	TOO MUCH
Insensitive No opportunities to witness Turn people off	Relaxed Good friendships Positive witness	Compromise Condone sin Encourage others to sin

Being Critical

KEY CONCEPT: Condemning others shows a lack of understanding.
GOAL: To replace faultfinding and nitpicking with positive expectations and hope.

Faultfinding is a common attempt to hide a lack of understanding. It reveals itself in nitpicking, ridiculing, or false accusations. Even words of praise with an insincere undertone can show disdain.

Understanding keeps you from having a critical attitude. Instead of assuming that every speeding car bears a reckless driver, the understanding person considers other possibilities for excessive speed, such as an emergency. The understanding person realizes that causes lie behind all behavior. Instead of being critical of actions, he or she says, "If I were that person, I might behave in the same way."

1. Be sure everyone knows that "critical" is used in this lesson in the negative sense of faultfinding.

2. Launching question: "Is it all right for me to judge someone if I am willing to be judged by the same standard? For example, can I say that a person was wrong for being drunk, if I am willing to be judged in the same way?"

3. "Can you think of an example of this principle?"

   "What are some ways you've seen this principle in your own life?"

5. "What are the implications of evaluating others by yourself?"

   "Why is it practiced so commonly?"

8. "Are there additional reasons not mentioned in this verse?"

9. "In 1 Samuel, the people made the tallest and strongest man king. What mistakes does judging people by appearances cause today?"

   "Since only God can look at the heart, and we can't, what are some clues that help you know people?"

10. "In context, Jesus said these words to Pharisees who criticized Him for healing on the Sabbath. In what ways do we, like Pharisees, criticize people wrongly?"

TEACHING IDEA: Arrange ahead of time for people to act out the following situations. After each one, ask the group for reasons that make the action understandable.

▶ A person talks loudly to another. (May be hard of hearing.)
▶ A person falls asleep during a church service. (May have been up all night or may be ill.)
▶ A person laughs inappropriately. (May be laughing at something else.)

The demonstration shows how understanding can keep you from being critical.

UNDERSTANDING 7
Discernment

KEY CONCEPT: Discernment from God is for helping others.
GOAL: To trust the Spirit of God to give discernment.

Criticism needs to be eliminated, and you need to consider hidden aspects that lie below surface appearances. The proper attitude is seen in Solomon—an understanding person understands his or her lack of understanding.

This means that though we should continuously work at understanding others, we cannot rely on our own ability. We must rely on God and look to Him to give discernment.

1. "What can we learn from these good examples that will help us have good discernment?"

2. "How can we know if our judgment agrees with God's?"

3. "How can you be a spiritual person as spoken of in verse 15?"

   "Who is the 'man without the Spirit' referred to in verse 14?"

5. There are at least four possible answers to this question, all of which have practical applications for us today.

6. "These two lists seem so radically different. Shouldn't there be a third list in between them? Explain."

   "Give an example of human-based wisdom."

7. "What are some bad fruits?"

   "What are some good fruits?"

   "Is everyone who has bad fruits bad? Explain."

   "Is everyone who has some good fruits good? Explain."

8. "Why do you think this helps you make better judgments?"

9. "Has there ever been a time in your life when someone came to you in this manner? Tell about it."

   "Was there ever a time in your life when someone should have? If so, tell what you think would have happened had you been approached."

TEACHING IDEA: Prepare two large cards. On one write "Spirit of God" and "Word of God." On the other write "Logic," "Mind," and "Experience." Ask one person to stand in front of the group with the

"Spirit of God" and "Word of God" card. Ask another to hold the other card. The first person will have God-sent discernment, the second will have human-based discernment. Then distribute index cards to the group. On each card should be written one characteristic from James 3:13-18. Ask the people who receive the cards to give their card to the correct person standing in front of the group.

Understanding Others' Convictions

KEY CONCEPT: Agreement on certain issues is not necessary for good relationships, love, and cooperation.

GOAL: To maintain right attitudes toward people with different convictions without debating the issues.

Churches may differ in governing systems, modes of baptism, and other doctrinal issues. Christians hold different ideas about many teachings and behaviors. In Paul's day, some ate meat sacrificed to idols and some felt it was wrong. Today, other controversies exist.

Whether dealing with teaching or behavior, everyone thinks his or her view is correct. People confidently assume others would agree with them if they understood the issues in the same way. But, no matter how long you study, you will not resolve all doctrinal and behavioral questions. Even so, you can gain an understanding of the people whose ideas differ from yours.

1-10. Be sure to focus the discussion on the proper way to react to those with differing convictions, not on debating controversies.

   3. The issues of Paul's day are not the major issues today. This question will help make this study relevant to the group. Ask group members to give their answers without identifying their convictions about the issues.

   4. "How does a 'partaker' who has the wrong attitude toward a 'nonpartaker' reflect that attitude in what he or she says?"

   "Paul stated the attitude in negative terms, saying not to look down on 'nonpartakers.' How can we state the proper attitude in positive terms?"

   "Why didn't Paul use the positive instead of the negative?"

   6. "How does a 'nonpartaker' who has the wrong attitude toward a 'partaker' reflect that attitude in what he or she says?"

   8. "Were there any attitudes you listed that surprised you somewhat? Which ones? Why?"

   10. "Paul could have moderated a debate on this issue. When do you find that debating the issues is really helpful to you?"

   "When is a debate destructive?"

TEACHING IDEA: On the chalkboard draw two faces with a piece of meat between them, slightly higher than the faces. When the faces consider the meat (draw a dotted line), one says, "Good," and the other says, "Bad." Now draw a dotted line from one face to the other, indicating they are considering each other, not the meat. Write in the correct attitudes for each face from questions 3, 4, and 5.

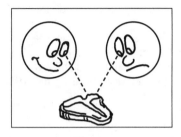 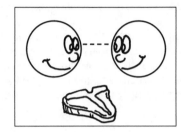

UNDERSTANDING **9**
Sensitivity to Others' Convictions

KEY CONCEPT: Scriptural guidelines should be followed in determining behavior not specified in the Bible.

GOAL: To restrict your liberties as an expression of love for others.

When two people sincerely hold different beliefs about an issue, the right attitudes are necessary to ensure understanding and lack of conflict. The attitude hurdle is a formidable barrier, but overcoming it is still not enough. We need to add loving and sensitive actions. These are the hallmarks of a truly understanding person.

1. "Is it necessary to agree to be sensitive?"

   "When there is disagreement, how does a sensitive person handle it?"

2. Be sure people list only those items that the Scriptures specifically say are wrong. Do not twist an application to a current issue not mentioned in Scripture.

   "What are some practices that many consider wrong but are not specified as such in the Bible?"

4. "Should we generalize commands like 'Do not be drunk' to 'Don't use drugs'? If so, who sets the limits on these generalizations?"

   Assume that an acceptable behavior is practiced in the correct way. (Anything can be wrong if it becomes an obsession that keeps you from other responsibilities.)

6. "How have these factors (or guidelines) been helpful to you in deciding whether or not to do a specific activity?"

7. "What should you do when it is not possible to please everyone around you?"

   "If someone is displeased with your behavior, have you automatically offended him or her in the scriptural sense? Explain."

8. "How can your liberties help you build relationships with nonbelievers?"

TEACHING IDEA: Draw a large, simple picture of a television and point out that the Bible doesn't mention television. Hand out seven cards, with one reference from question 6 on each. The people receiving the cards should look up the reference and write on their card one criterion that should be used in determining whether watching television is right or wrong. Then ask the seven people to come to the front of the group and tape their cards on the board while explaining each criterion.

40

HONORING

Seeing Value in Others

KEY CONCEPT: The foundation of value in people is in having been created in God's image.

GOAL: To recognize the intrinsic value in others in such a way as to regard them with respect.

James warned believers in the first century not to show favoritism toward the wealthy (James 2:1-4). Today he would probably include sport figures, movie stars, singers, models, and politicians in the warning. James was not suggesting that these people are not worthy of respect, but rather that those not in these categories are worthy of equal respect.

To many, the person with money has value. The fast runner has value. The gracious and charismatic actor has value. The good singer has value. Those who create public policy have value. But most people don't fit into any of these categories. We need to see from God's perspective to appreciate the value in people.

1. "How is this value system used by people in general?"

   "What are some of the effects of this value system?"

2. "What can help us keep mindful of this truth?"

3. "What are some ways all people are like God?"

   "What are some of the ways all believers are like God?"

5. "Imagine if you could have been there when Jesus said this. How would you have reacted?"

   "Would you have considered these men to have greater value than they did before Jesus said this?"

6. "Should we always think Jesus sees value in us? Explain."

   "What, if anything, can be done to see more value in ourselves?"

7. "In what ways are you like John?"

8. Ask group members to contribute as many ideas as possible without any evaluations.

10. "What are some of the things that happen in you when others see value in you?"

TEACHING IDEA: One of the most important foundations of esteeming and honoring is that people bear the image of God (question 2). Bring a flag to class to illustrate honoring the image. We salute the flag and honor it, not because of the cloth or the colors, but because it represents the country. In a similar way, we honor people because they are a "flag" of God even when dirty, torn, or tattered.

HONORING **2**
Honoring Leaders

KEY CONCEPT: Honoring leaders begins in prayer.
GOAL: To respect the dignity of positions of leadership at work, at church, and in government.

There are special directives to give honor to those who are in positions of leadership. Giving them honor is not the same as approving all their actions, values, or ideals.

Throughout history, many believers have lived under the rule of atheists and idolaters. These leaders' erroneous ideas about God do not relieve our responsibility to honor them. We honor leaders because God has placed them in their positions.

1. "What difference, if any, is there in honoring leaders as opposed to honoring people in general?"

   "To you personally, what is the most important aspect of honor?"

2. Encourage the group members to go beyond an answer of "everyone" by asking for specific groups of people who should be honored.

   "What do you consider proper respect (as mentioned in 1 Peter 2:17)?"

3. Contrast Proverbs 20:3 with current television or movie heroes who are "honored" because they use violence for the sake of justice by asking, "According to Proverbs 20:3, should we honor people like _____? Explain." (Fill in the blank with a current hero.)

4. "First Samuel 2:30 was spoken to Eli. How had Eli failed to honor God?"

5. Evaluate the following ideas about honor in your church fellowship: appreciation banquets, trophies with inscriptions, name plaques on pews, a note of thanks, a smile.

6. If people list a category instead of individual names, ask for specific names.

7. "Consider the case of Dan, who has held nineteen jobs over the last twelve years (fifteen of them were career-type employment). Do you think he has problems honoring his bosses? Explain."

   "What questions do you think Dan should face about his own life?"

8. "Are you honoring leaders if you confront them about weaknesses in their lives?"

44

"If so, how can you do it effectively?"

10. "What kind of leader was Saul?"

    "What aspects of his life would have made it difficult for you to honor him?"

TEACHING IDEA: Start the session with an announcement: "We have a special guest today. Would everyone please rise and welcome _____." (Use the name of some local leader.)

After waiting for a few seconds, tell the group you were only giving an example of honoring a leader by having them rise. Then ask them why they were happy to show honor by rising.

Make three columns on the chalkboard and title them "Who," "Why," and "How." As you cover the material in this lesson, enter a summary of the information in the appropriate column(s).

Honoring Family Members

KEY CONCEPT: Honor your parents, your spouse, your children.

GOAL: To highly regard the rights of other family members without demanding your own.

Perhaps the easiest place to forget to honor one another is in the home. Husbands who neglect their wives are not honoring them. Wives who complain about their husbands are not honoring them. Parents who fail to consider the thoughts and feelings of their children are not honoring them. Children who rebel against parents are not honoring them.

Homes without honor are homes in chaos.

1. Suggest that group members do this exercise with everyone in the family participating. Ask any who have already done this to tell about the experience.

2. Encourage your group to apply the principle from the question further. For example, if you conclude, "Familiarity erodes respect," you should give special care to honor people you know well—like your spouse.

3. "What suggestions do you have for teaching children to honor their parents without creating a formal and distant relationship?"

4. "Does honoring our parents include financial responsibility for elderly parents and/or grandparents? Explain."

5. "What are some ways to 'save up' for your children in spiritual and intellectual ways, as well as tangible ways?"

6. "What are some specific opportunities for publicly endorsing your children?"

7. "Men, what do you think your wives regard as the most important ways for you to honor them?"

   "Wives, are they right?"

8. "Women, what do you think your husbands regard as the most important ways for you to honor them?"

   "Husbands, are they right?"

TEACHING IDEA: Draw stick figures as in the illustration that follows, leaving space to write under them. As you lead the discussion about honoring parents, draw in the arrow from the children to the parents and write a summary of questions 3 and 4 under "Honor Parents." Then draw the arrow from the parents to the children and write a summary of questions 5 and 6 under "Honor Children." Finally, draw the arrow between the parents and write a summary of questions 7 and 8 under "Honor Spouse."

Deferring to Others

KEY CONCEPT: Others' interests take higher priority than your own.
GOAL: To consider others' needs instinctively, not your own.

To honor others means giving them priority in your values. When you demand your rights, you imply you are to be esteemed and your needs met. By putting others first, you allow others' needs to be met.

At times, this is as simple as letting the other person tell his or her story while you listen. Other times the "cost" can be greater.

1. "How important are these 'little things'?"

   "How do we defer to others in larger ways?"

2. "Do the reasons given in this passage motivate you to put others first? If not, what does?"

3,4. "How would you word these principles for people today?" (Use for both old and new principles.)

3. "Jesus gave these instructions to people under the rule of a foreign power. Do you think He would say the same thing to us today? Explain."

3c. "Who in this group has been sued? How do you feel about these instructions?"

   "Who has been forced to help someone? How do you feel about that?"

4b. "Wouldn't applying this principle be disastrous to a businessperson? Explain."

5. "What benefits do you reap when you obey Jesus' commands?"

6. There are many instances when seeking a person's good would not include deferring to his or her desires.

7. "It is easy to tell what is the right thing to do in situations like this. It is an altogether different matter actually to do the right thing. What should we do to prepare ourselves to do the right thing?"

8. Ask all the people who chose Abraham to tell what lessons they learned, then those who chose Jacob, and so on.

TEACHING IDEA: Bring three or four children's building blocks to class. Line them up in front of the group and ask which block is first. Some may think the one on the right is, others may think the one on the left is. It is a matter of perspective. In the same way, when we put others first, it may appear that we are at the end of the line, but God says we've moved to the head of the line.

Serving Others

KEY CONCEPT: Serving others is a privilege and the way to true
greatness.
GOAL: To serve without anticipating rewards or gratitude.

One characteristic of faith is seeing from a divine perspective. To the natural eye, it appears that slaves are inferior to their masters. But God says
they can be greater than their masters without leaving the ranks of slavery. You can become great in God's economy no matter what your position, job, title, or finances.

Serving is God's way to become great. But if we serve only to
become great and not because we esteem others as being worthy of being
served, we defeat our own service. We must assume the *role* of a servant,
not merely perform some duties.

1. "What can we do to make serving everyone more enjoyable?"

2. "Many people have the same kind of thoughts as James and John
   but don't verbalize them. What are some ways people reveal that
   they think they are great?"

2c. "Why do you think the disciples failed to learn the lesson the first
   time?"

   "How are we like them?"

3. "If you had been one of the Twelve, how do you think it would have
   felt as Jesus washed your feet?"

4. "What wrong attitudes or actions do you think Jesus was trying to
   correct with this teaching?"

5. Luke 17:10 expresses the view you should have toward yourself.
   Matthew 25:21 expresses the view the Lord has toward some of His
   servants.

6. "What are the best characteristics of this servant?"

   "What are the worst?"

   "In what ways do you identify with the servant?"

   "How can following the servant's example improve your service?"

7. "Are the reasons we've listed always apparent to us? Why, or why
   not?"

8. "What is it about an unreasonable boss that makes us want to
   rebel?"

9. "This principle indicates small responsibilities should be given before major ones are assigned. How can we do this in running Sunday school? In church government?"

10. "How can serving others open opportunities to talk about the gospel?"

"Should we continue to serve others if opportunities to discuss the gospel do not develop? Why, or why not?"

11. "What is one example of the sowing/reaping principle?"

TEACHING IDEA: Write "Greatness" on a large chart and, from question 2, show that there is nothing wrong with a desire to be great. Write "Men's ideas" at the bottom and put in ideas you gathered in your study. As you write each one, draw an arrow that misses "Greatness" (see diagram). Write "God's idea," read Matthew 20:28, and show that serving "hits" greatness.

Humility Before God

KEY CONCEPT: God befriends the humble and not the arrogant.
GOAL: To walk in dependence upon God and appreciation for all He has
done.

The humble person does not suffer from feelings of inferiority even in
relationship to God. Though God is superior, He does not delight in making us feel inferior. He elevates us by making us in His image, by
dwelling in us, and by making us His heirs.

God also does not delight in those who forget that this position is
God's gift to us. If we boast as though we had done it ourselves, we are
not humble before Him. If we think this position gives us rights we can
demand, we are not humble before Him. If we treat Him as an equal, we
are not humble before Him.

2. "What characteristics, in addition to those mentioned in these passages, do you associate with humility before God?"

4. "What relationship do you see between these three actions?"

5. These verses are difficult to correlate to some other passages. Keep
   the discussion focused on humility before God.

   "What other reasons are there for humility before God?"

6. "Which of the blessings you listed do you appreciate most?"

   "Do you see a cause-and-effect relationship between the blessing
   promised and humility?"

7. "What other actions do you associate with humility before God?"

8. "What do you consider to be your major personal obstacle?"

9. Use this exercise in a time of worship. Ask the participants to close
   their eyes and assume a worshipful attitude. Then one at a time
   ask each person to read his or her letter without any additional
   comments.

TEACHING IDEA: List the three actions from Micah 6:8 (question 4) in
front of the group as illustrated. Ask the group to give other actions or
attitudes that go with these. Some possible responses are written in the
diagram. After completing this, review God's promises from question 6.

LOVE JUSTICE	SHOW MERCY	WALK HUMBLY
Be honest	Forgive	Have faith
Be fair	Have patience	Be spirit-controlled

Humility Before Others

KEY CONCEPT: Humility is possible when you walk in the Spirit.
GOAL: To reflect a humble attitude in actions toward others.

Many consider humility to be a type of self-abasement. Actually, it is having an accurate view of yourself. When you have a correct self-image, you can look up to others without feeling inferior.

The humble person finds it easy to esteem others and easily opens doors for relationships with them. Humility builds trust and cooperation, arrogance feeds competition and strife. Humility eases tension, arrogance breeds arguments. Humility listens and understands, arrogance prejudges and criticizes. Humility builds others up, arrogance tears them down. No greater tool for building positive relationships has been found than humility.

1. "Rarely is anyone so blatant as we have been in this game. How do people actually play the 'That's Nothing' game?"

2. "What characteristics, in addition to those derived from these passages, do you associate with humility?"

3. "What other common ideas about humility can be shown wrong by Jesus' example?"

   "Which of the characteristics of humility do you feel is most difficult to demonstrate in our society?"

4. "What can we conclude about who Jesus thought He was from the statement in verse 6?"

   "For you, when is it easiest to release your grasp on your position—when you feel secure or insecure? Why?"

   "In what sense does Paul mean, 'Your attitude should be the same as that of Christ Jesus'? How can we do it? Are there any practical steps?"

5. "In what ways is a child humble?"

   "In what ways is a child not humble?"

6. "What do you think happens when God opposes you?"

   "What does God say will happen when we apply this principle?"

   "In light of these verses, what 'care' do you think is being talked about in 1 Peter 5:7?"

9. "Has anyone experienced this or seen it happen to someone else?"

    "What would happen differently if the seat of honor were taken by a misunderstanding as opposed to being taken on purpose?"

10. "Did Naaman have real humility, or did he have a 'no harm in trying' attitude?"

    "Naaman's lack of humility was shown when his expectations weren't fulfilled. What other things often reveal a lack of humility?"

    "Wasn't Elisha impolite by not seeing Naaman?"

11. "What experiences have you had that helped you become more humble?"

    "In what ways is humility easier to maintain as you get older?"

    "In what ways is it more difficult?"

12. "Do these advantages motivate you to be humble? If so, how? If not, what does motivate you to be humble?"

TEACHING IDEA: Enlist people ahead of time to act out the two scenes from question 9. You will need to develop your own dialogue. As they act it out, ask the actors to also tell the audience what they are thinking. For example, "I see the best seat is vacant; it must be for me. Who else would sit there?" Then ask the group what the skit teaches.

Learning from Others

KEY CONCEPT: Teachability involves realizing your ignorance, listening to others, and applying what is right.

GOAL: To listen and learn from others without becoming gullible or skeptical.

Someone said, "You don't have to take a man's advice to make him feel good; all you have to do is ask for it." Learning from another is one of the surest signs of esteem. It shows you value that person's ideas and judgments.

Pride keeps you from learning from others because you are enamored with your own ideas. They are trying to pour diamonds into a bucket already filled with stones. But when you empty yourself of preconceived notions, you can consider others' ideas honestly.

1. "What is the trick to learning from poor teachers?"

3. "I'm sure we all are confident that we know something. How should we apply 1 Corinthians 8:2?"

   "Why do people often *not* hear while they are listening?"

4. "What kinds of things can we learn from unrighteous people?"

6. "What can help you make accurate observations?"

7. "Notice the balance in their lives. They were neither gullible nor skeptical. What can keep us from these extremes?"

8. "What have you seen other people do because they thought someone was unteachable?"

   "What should you do if you have a teachable attitude but others don't think you do?"

TEACHING IDEA: Draw a scale like the illustration below and write "Unteachable" and "Gullible" above it. Ask the group to suggest words describing these two extremes. Point out the balance presented in Acts 17:11.

Accepting Correction

KEY CONCEPT: Reproof demonstrates a person's high esteem of you and can benefit your life.

GOAL: To listen patiently to reproof and apply true and scriptural teachings.

1. "How do people usually regard correction from those who do not fulfill the qualifications we've discussed?"

2. "What are some other benefits of accepting reproof?"

3. "Do you think most people who have reproved you have had this evaluation of you? Why, or why not?"

4. "Do you believe God is in control of a wrong reproof? Do your actions reflect this belief?"

5. "Many 'reproofs' are done in the wrong way by irate supervisors unleashing their frustrations. What is a good model of reproof?"

   "How can reproof be handled without discouraging the person being reproved?"

6. "What are some other types of correction?"

   "When are they appropriate?"

7. "What other 'tests' should we use to identify false teachers?"

   Help the participants in their evaluations. They should consider a person a false teacher only if he or she is teaching something definitely contrary to Scripture, not merely a different idea from theirs.

8. "From what you studied in 2 Peter 2, what are some strong indications that a person is a false teacher?"

   "How do you think false teachers should be handled?"

TEACHING IDEA: Act out the reproof of some of the situations below. In one case be overly harsh. In another be so gentle the person doesn't know correction took place.

▶ A person wears inappropriate clothing.
▶ A person fails to fulfill a pledge to do a job.
▶ You overhear a person instruct a fellow church member using wrong concepts.
▶ You are attempting to help a Sunday school teacher improve his or her teaching techniques.

SUBMITTING

The Sovereignty of God

KEY CONCEPT: God has absolute authority.
GOAL: To be at peace with human authority because God is in charge.

Consider how you would normally react to two librarians, one who snarls, "Will you shut up?" and one who smiles and gently says, "Please, don't disturb others." Both are asking you to do the same thing, and most people would oblige both—but with different feelings.

One reason for the difference in your reaction is how you perceive the authority being exercised. Submission is easier when you see a kind, loving overseer. So, when we realize our loving Father is behind all authority, submission is easier, even when the message is harsh.

1. "Is 'sovereign' a synonym for 'God'?"

2. "Does this mean God controlled the election of our president? If so, why vote? If not, in what sense does He create rulers?"

3. "When, if ever, do you feel God is not in control?"

   Warning: Some people in your group may have difficulty accepting the sovereignty of God because they think it would remove our choice of action and, consequently, our responsibility. The Bible clearly teaches both God's sovereignty and our responsibility. Make sure your group understands you are studying only God's sovereignty and that no one should assume he or she does not have a choice or responsibility.

4. "Are God's purposes in regard to the spread of the gospel being fulfilled? Explain."

5. "How can we use the authority of God's Word in our daily conversations with others?"

6. "What are some things people pray about that indicate they don't have confidence in God's sovereignty?"

8. "In what ways do you identify with Job as he expresses his feelings in these passages?"

9. If the response "every way" is given, ask for specific ways.

   "What are some of the implications of God's control over these issues?"

Conclude your discussion with a time of thanking and praising God for His sovereignty.

TEACHING IDEA: Present the concept of Colossians 1:16-17, following the diagram. First, write "Colossians 1:16-17" and "All Things," and ask the group to look at the reference. Write "Definition" on the first column and show that "All Things" means anything in Heaven or earth and anything visible or invisible. Write "Examples" on the second column and list the things included in "All Things": thrones, dominions, principalities, and powers (all are authority positions). Write "Statements" on the third column and list the four statements: all things created by God; all things are for God; all things exist by Him; and He is before all things.

COLOSSIANS 1:16-17—ALL THINGS

DEFINITION	EXAMPLES	STATEMENTS
1. Anything in Heaven or earth 2. Anything visible or invisible	1. Thrones 2. Dominions 3. Principalities 4. Powers	1. All things created by God 2. All things are for God 3. All things exist by Him 4. He is before all things

The Nature of Submission

KEY CONCEPT: Submit to those in authority as unto God.

GOAL: To have a wholehearted desire to fulfill the directives of those in authority.

There is a philosophy that advocates conditioning the human race for blind submission to law and order. Its advocates maintain that the elimination of freedom and dignity in people will be offset by the overall good that results.

God's plan for you includes a submission that does not remove individuality, freedom, or dignity. Rather than transforming you into a robot programed for obedience, He wants you to submit lovingly to the Holy Spirit in you and to people He has put over you.

1. "Did you find you almost automatically began thinking of negative experiences? If so, why do you suppose this happened?"

2. Ask group members to present their concepts without discussion. Use your discussion time for the conclusions given in the next question.

3. "How can we combine the concepts of individual responsibility with submitting to others?"

4. "Which of the two sons are you like most of the time?"

   "What do most people think about each of the two sons?"

5. "In your experience how have people reacted to you when you question a directive?"

   "What have you learned is the best way to question a directive?"

6. "What helps you maintain spiritual mindedness?"

8. "What other benefits are there in submitting?"

9. "If submitting does not eliminate your frustration in a given situation, what should you do?"

TEACHING IDEA: Write "Submission" on a large chart and make three columns under it titled "Attitude," "Intent," and "Action." Write what you learn in the appropriate column as you cover the material. It will be evident that it is not easy to maintain the right attitude, the right intent, and the right actions all the time. To do this, we must be spiritually minded. Draw a horizontal line under the three columns and write "Spiritually Minded" under it to represent the foundation of submission.

Good Leadership

KEY CONCEPT: Righteousness and the fear of God are essential to good leadership.

GOAL: To be diligent, impartial, and righteous in exercising any position of authority.

The harmonious relationship God desires between a person in authority and a person under authority exists when both people fulfill the responsibilities God has given them. The oppressive nature of misused authority creates tension and encourages rebelliousness.

Most people have positions of authority as well as positions under authority. Obeying God's directives for positions of authority and under authority minimizes tension, encourages cooperation, and enables you to accomplish your objectives.

1. "Does a person have to be a believer to be an effective leader? Explain."

2. "How would you describe sunrise on a cloudless day?"

   "How does viewing it make you feel?"

   "What other comparisons would you make to illustrate effective leadership?"

3. "Are there additional qualities you consider essential to good leadership?"

5. "What types of oppression have you seen by parents? By elders? By bosses? By teachers?"

   "What problems did this cause?"

6. "How can we generalize this command for greater application?"

7. "What is one specific action you can take in applying this verse to your position?"

8a. "What are some additional wrong motives people have for seeking leadership positions?"

TEACHING IDEA: Hand several objects to people in the group, making sure everyone either has an object or is sitting near someone who does. Some of the objects have no intended significance. Choose other items that can represent the character traits from questions 1 and 2. For example, you can use:

▶ a Bible to represent ruling in the fear of God.

▶ a ruler to represent impartiality because it measures all things the same way.

▶ a penny to represent honesty because it is inscribed with a picture of "Honest Abe."

As you go through each character trait for leaders listed in questions 1 and 2, tell the group that among the objects you passed out, there is at least one that represents this character trait. Then ask as many people as possible to give their ideas on how one of the objects represents the trait. Don't be surprised if they have ideas that are new to you.

The Responsibility of Leaders

KEY CONCEPT: As a leader you are a representative of God.
GOAL: To exercise authority to serve and protect those who follow.

The character traits of a leader reflect his or her spiritual state and development. These requisites qualify a person to have leadership, but do not automatically mean the leader will exercise it properly.

Even those who do not wish to use their position for power, glory, or money may fail to use it properly. Authority is a responsibility to serve. And a primary focus of your service should be those you supervise. Parents serve children, bosses serve employees, teachers serve students—this promotes perfected relationships.

1. "When do you prefer leading?"

   "When do you prefer following?"

2. "What are some ways this concern should affect those of us who are parents? Teachers?"

3. "How are followers like sheep? How are they not like them?"

   "Because we are not too familiar with shepherding, what are some ways of illustrating these principles using modern examples?"

4. "Who is the wolf? The hired hand?"

   "Does paying a minister a salary make him a hired hand? If not, what does?"

5b. "Is every action Paul lists in 1 Thessalonians 2 a way of serving people? Why, or why not?"

   "When and why should a leader serve his followers by washing dishes, shining shoes, or sweeping the floor?"

7. "Paul's comments in 1 Timothy 3:1 indicate we should desire authority. James' warning indicates we should not. What is a balanced view?"

8. "What is one specific action you can take to serve someone under you?"

TEACHING IDEA: Bring refreshments to class and, instead of teaching, serve the group refreshments. Don't comment about why you are doing this; just continue to do acts of service. Continue until someone asks, "When are we going to begin?" You can reply, "I began teaching ten minutes ago." Ask what the group liked about it, what they didn't like, what was good and what was bad. Use the responses to catapult you into the ideas from the lesson.

Submitting at Work

KEY CONCEPT: Submit to your boss as long as you are employed.
GOAL: To perform your duties at work and protect those who follow.

Job and career are more personal than government, and submission on
the job can be a more emotional subject. People who work hard often
have ideas they feel would help their employers. At times, these good
ideas get scuttled by an insecure boss. The lack of consideration for the
ideas can result in resentment, making submission difficult.

1. "What are some factors that make work unenjoyable?"

   "How can we put joy into unenjoyable work?"

3. "Is there ever a situation when you should not submit? If so,
   when?"

4. "A person might maintain these standards and get criticized for
   having a 'holier-than-thou' attitude. How should you handle this?"

5. "Money is one issue that creates conflict at work. What are other
   issues?"

   "Would a submissive spirit keep these issues from becoming
   conflicts?"

6. "What else can we do instead of complaining?"

   "What does Scripture say about complaining?" Ask the group to
   look up Philippians 2:14 and Hebrews 13:5.

7. "Complaining to the wrong people rarely does any good. Why do
   we tend to do this?"

9. "At a company picnic, you mention an idea you have to the president. He seems to like it and asks you to pursue it. Later, at work,
   your direct supervisor rejects the idea. You feel going directly to the
   president will cause problems and prompt your boss to 'get you' for
   'going over his head.' What would you do?"

10. "At the office people say you have to play golf with the boss at least
    once to get a promotion—and your experience confirms that. You
    feel you deserve a promotion but you don't like golf. Would you ask
    God to exercise His authority as expressed in Psalm 75:6-7, or
    would you play golf with the boss? Why?"

TEACHING IDEA: This exercise should help members see the benefits of
submitting at work.

Divide the group into smaller groups of three to five. Half of the groups will represent employers and half, employees. Employer groups should answer the following, using the reference in question 2.

► "What attitude(s) does the passage say you should have?"
► "How would you, as an employer, respond to an employee with this attitude(s)?"
► "How would you respond to an employee without this attitude(s)?"

At the same time the employees should answer the questions from an employee's standpoint. After five minutes, ask a representative from each group to give a short report.

Submitting to Government

KEY CONCEPT: God places civil authority over you for your benefit.
GOAL: To obey the laws of the land wholeheartedly.

In the Old Testament, civil government and spiritual leadership were often intertwined and sometimes one in the same. Some of the directives God gave Moses apply both as moral dictates and as civil law. When these two types of leadership are united, submission to God means submission to His appointed leaders.

The New Testament was created in a different political environment. Believers were virtually all under Roman rule, and submitting to this theologically unsound and morally bankrupt government was not easy.

1. "Why do governments and government officials so often tend to be immoral?"

3b. "What can you do when it seems that these purposes are not being accomplished?"

4c. "What will enable you to have the right attitude when paying your taxes?"

5. "What should you do when it seems that your interests are not being protected?"

6. "In a historical novel about the Russian Revolution, masses of people are being herded aboard a train to be relocated in concentration camps. Only one man is shackled. He lifts his chained hands in front of his face and yells, 'I'm the only free man!' Is he? How? How is that like the freedom we have in Christ?"

7b. Things that Jesus did not do are mentioned in 1 Peter 2:23. Discuss with your group some typical ways people do these things today. For example, Jesus did not revile. Today some revile others by name-calling. Then discuss ways to follow Jesus' example.

8a. "What are some examples of directives that should not be obeyed?"

8b. "What are some examples of directives that we would rather not obey but should?"

10. "Since Jesus is the King's son, He was not obliged to pay the tax. Yet He did. When should we submit to laws that technically do not apply to us?"

TEACHING IDEA: Prepare a short skit ahead of time with two other members of the group. Begin leading the session, and have the other two burst in and arrest you for no reason. They should pretend to do this in a very rough manner, supposedly beating you up and dragging you off. After it's over, ask the other group members how they would feel if they lived under a government where actions like this could happen. Point out that the authorities existing in New Testament times did things like that. It was in this historical context that Paul wrote Romans 13. Continue to teach the concepts from question 4.

Submitting in the Family

KEY CONCEPT: Submission in the family assures smooth relationships.
GOAL: To use submission for the benefit and order of the family unit.

Too often people tend to focus attention on dysfunctional families instead of on model families. Submission is not meant to be a tool to suppress others, but to allow the family to function as a unit. Without authority and submission, anarchy prevails and power is centered in the strong, the clever manipulator, or the deceiver.

1. "What have been some of the most enjoyable and beneficial aspects of your family?"

2. "How can we help our children learn to obey?"

   "How can we help friends who have disobedient children?"

3. "It is likely that some people regarded Jesus' actions as rebellious or disobedient. When do you think you should 'wink' at actions instead of being strict?"

4. "Eli's children were no longer youngsters. What responsibility do you think Eli should have had for their behavior? Why?"

5. Help the people in your group establish specific plans rather than general ideas. For example, if one says he is going to teach his children God's Word, help him establish a definite plan as to when he is going to teach, what he is going to teach, etc.

7. "To what does 'in the same way' (verse 1) refer?"

8. "Are there any ways you think Sarah is a bad example?"

9. "What are some specific situations where you think a husband should submit to his wife?"

   "What are some general principles we can conclude from these specifics?"

TEACHING IDEAS: For question 6, give everyone two pieces of paper. Ask group members to write "my responsibilities" on one and "my spouse's responsibilities" on the other. (Singles should do the exercise as though they were married.) Give them three to five minutes to complete lists from Ephesians 5:21-28. Afterward, ask them to tear up "my spouse's responsibilities" to illustrate they shouldn't "check up" on their spouse. They should keep the "my responsibilities" list as a reminder.
   Ask everyone in the group to write a response to question 5 on a

piece of paper. Encourage them to make practical suggestions rather than general ideas. For example, "Take your children one at a time out for a special dinner once a month" is better than "Establish better communications." Other ideas may include the titles of books for parents to read alone or with their children, ideas for developing their children's gifts, etc. After everyone has written an idea on a piece of paper, ask the people to pass the papers around. Parents should glance at the ideas and pass them on until they find an idea they think would be especially useful. They should keep this piece of paper.

Submitting to Spiritual Leaders

KEY CONCEPT: Spiritual leaders are appointed to watch over God's flock.

GOAL: To gain the benefits of having spiritual leaders by submitting to them.

The church consists of all believers in Jesus Christ. Some are babes in Christ, others are young Christians, and others are mature. From mature Christians come church leaders.

Leaders, like shepherds, have responsibilities to watch, protect, feed, and guide the "sheep" placed in their care.

To receive the full benefits of the shepherd's care, sheep must cooperate by submitting to his or her leadership. There are penalties for ignoring the government's authority—for example, being fined for filing a false tax return. There are also penalties for ignoring the spiritual authority God has placed over us. If people take their leaders too casually, they may end up fighting against God.

1. "Which leader do you look to for comfort? For advice? For challenge?"

2. "When you have these attitudes, who benefits the most, you or the leader? Explain."

3. "When, if ever, should you oppose a spiritual leader?"

   "How should you do this?"

   "Why do you think Jesus put greater emphasis on our responsibility to obey a spiritual leader than on correcting the leader's problems?"

4. "How would you rephrase these commands in modern language?"

5. "In what way do we become like our leaders?"

   "In what ways do we not become like them?"

6. After each member has read his or her response ask, "How can we hold one another accountable for these commitments?"

7. "What if your pastor asked you to quit your job to work as an associate at church?"

9. "How important do you think an armor-bearer (sidekick) is to effective spiritual leadership?"

   "What can we do to equip ourselves to be effective armor-bearers?"

TEACHING IDEA: Make arrangements for someone to interrupt the group meeting shortly after its beginning to give you a message from the pastor. "The pastor would like you to come to his office immediately. He knows you are leading this group, but this is important. The group will have to fend for itself."

Then excuse yourself from the group and walk out. After a few seconds, return to the meeting and ask for reactions to what happened. After presenting the lesson, ask if going to the pastor's office would have been the correct response if you had actually been summoned.

CONTRIBUTING

Having Spiritual Gifts

KEY CONCEPT: God has gifted every believer for the good of all.

GOAL: To recognize that you have gifts that are needed for the Body of Christ to function properly.

You have a contribution to make to the Body of Christ because God has equipped you with gifts.

It is not prideful to appreciate the gifts God has given you. It is part of a rational self-view. The person who claims to be worthless is expressing pride. His view focuses on self and not on God, who has given gifts.

The mature Christian will recognize his or her gifts and use them to help others in the Body in a way that improves relationships and expresses love.

1. "What makes people valuable to you?"

2. "Why do you think some people have a hard time recognizing that they have gifts?"

3. "When do you get a gift?"

4. This exercise can become boring if you belabor these lists. Ask four different people to read one of their lists, and then go on to discuss question 5.

5. "An illustrative list gives examples. An exhaustive list contains all possibilities. Are the combined lists from question 4 illustrative or exhaustive? Why?"

6. "How important is it to know your gift(s)? Why?"

7. "What else has given you insight into your gifts?"

8. If someone has difficulty determining his or her gift, ask the group to tell ways the person has contributed to them or others. Remind everyone that you don't need to identify your gifts to contribute to others.

9. "In what sense do the gifts God gives us need to be opened?"

   "How do we do it?"

TEACHING IDEA: Prepare gift labels for all the people in your group. The labels should say, "To the Church, with love, from the Holy Spirit. P.S. I know you need this." As people arrive for class, pin a tag on each one. Later, explain the tag: Each person is a gift from God, the Holy Spirit, to the rest of the Church, equipped to meet special needs in the Body.

Read the following responses to question 6 and ask the group to suggest possible gifts these statements indicate: Person A—"I enjoy doing things for others, especially fixing or building things. I'm good at carpentry, and most people like the cabinets I have built. They say I have a real knack in this area." Person B—"I enjoy getting to know people and drawing them out. I'm good at listening and finding out what's going on inside them. People seem to enjoy talking to me, and they say I am very understanding."

CONTRIBUTING 2
Using Spiritual Gifts

KEY CONCEPT: Your gift is necessary for the Church's well-being.
GOAL: To use your gifts without pride, a sense of superiority, or a sense of inferiority.

Knowing about gifts or even knowing your gifts is not enough. We all must use our gifts for the good of each other. This mutual contribution will build personal relationships as people grow spiritually.

Growing believers in healthy relationships are the backbone of a local church and enable it to function properly. This results in others being attracted to the fellowship, where they are contributed to and contribute to others.

1b. "What practical steps can we take to bring some of these dreams into reality?"

"What obstacles do we need to remove? How can we remove them?"

2. "Can you think of any other reasons why God has gifted us?"

3. "What do you consider to be a sane approach?"

"What can happen when people have a wrong view of themselves?"

4. "How can we know we are using the ability God has given us?"

5. "When a part of your body is hurt, how does the rest of your body respond?"

"How does this illustrate the way we should react to each other?"

6. "Describe a situation where the proper use of gifts has benefited *you*."

7. "Which do you think should be emphasized—the fruit of the Spirit or the gifts of the Spirit? Why?"

8. "What should you do if you do not feel important to our fellowship?"

TEACHING IDEA: Conduct a mock trial, giving directions to the participants (the defendant, whose name is "Liver"; the defense attorney; the prosecuting attorney; and the judge) in advance.

The case involves Liver wanting to withdraw from the body because he or she is not as attractive, prominent, or recognized as the beautiful hair, sparkling eyes, or muscular arms.

Liver is on the witness stand. The defense attorney argues the apparent "injustice" of Liver's position in the body. The prosecuting attorney argues that Liver is more dispensable than the more prominent parts of the body.

This should lead to the judge's verdict—the body can do without many parts, but not Liver. Liver is indispensable.

Then have a discussion making parallel applications to spiritual gifts and the Body of Christ.

Contributing with Good Works

KEY CONCEPT: Good works are an evidence, not a cause, of salvation.
GOAL: To perform good works without expecting them to earn you
  anything.

One of the surest signs that a person is walking with God is the evidence
of God's love flowing through the person in a continual stream of good
deeds. These deeds contribute to the lives of others as they are helped.
They contribute to relationships by creating good will. They contribute to
further opportunities to minister by opening doors of communication
and confidence.

Yet, the benefits of good works have a limit. They cannot earn a
place in Heaven for anyone.

2. Suggest a group project of providing a program of entertainment
   for the residents of a nursing home.

3. "What other benefits of good deeds are there?"

4. "Although this passage says salvation is not of ourselves, suppose it
   was. What would that imply about you? About God? About those
   who have not attained it?"

5. "Some people stop doing some good deeds because they feel
   abused. How can you keep from the sense of abuse?"

6. "What good deeds are especially useful in opening doors to communicate the gospel to nonChristians?"

7. "What are some other things that make us shine?"

8. "Why do you think having people come to your home is a strong
   factor in creating friendships?"

   "Why do many church members fail to invite nonbelievers to their
   homes?"

9. The verses listed after each situation create some tension by indicating that two different actions should be taken. There are creative
   ways to apply both teachings.

TEACHING IDEAS: Light a candle and silently watch it for about a
minute. Then comment, "It doesn't make a lot of noise does it?" Then
ask people to contribute other ideas on how to be like a candle.

Present the relationship of good works to salvation in questions 3
and 4 by using the following diagram. Draw the two circles and an arrow
from "good works" to "salvation." Ask people in the group to read

Scripture passages that show this is not true. Now erase the arrow between the circles and ask, "What is wrong with good works and salvation being totally separate from one another?" The participants may have a more difficult time answering this question, and you may need to point out the references from questions 3 and 4. Lastly, draw the arrow from salvation to good works to show that good works flow out of our salvation and that lack of good works may indicate a person is not really a Christian.

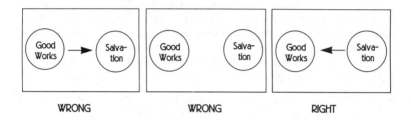

WRONG   WRONG   RIGHT

Contributing by Support

KEY CONCEPT: Mutual support should characterize God's people.
GOAL: To use your strengths to support those who do not have the same strengths.

Bill encouraged Frank when he was depressed about his Christian life. Frank gave Mary money to help pay her rent. Mary took care of Sally's children while Sally counseled and comforted Jill after her husband died. Jill typed some papers for Bill that he needed for the Sunday school class he taught.

Everyone supporting; everyone supported. All with something to offer. None sufficient alone. This is support in the Body of Christ.

1. "Which of you have received support from someone who would not be considered a particularly gifted individual?"

   "What qualifies a person to give support?"

2. "How do you feel about people who support you like this?"

   "When could too much support enable someone to be dependent or deprive him or her of independence?"

4. "What effect do negative comments such as complaining, gossip, and bitterness have on you?"

   "What effect do positive comments such as success stories, humor, or compliments have on you?"

5. "Give an example of these principles in action."

   "What application do these verses suggest to you?"

6. "What can we specifically do to fulfill this action?"

7. "Why do most people consider themselves to be 'the strong'?"

8. "Are we generally known for making people feel good about themselves or the opposite? What should we do about this?"

9. "Why should Gehazi have known that the woman was disturbed?"

   "Later, we discover that Gehazi was an unfaithful servant. What relationship do you think this has to his lack of sensitivity?"

10. "What are some needs you have that you have difficulty expressing to others?"

TEACHING IDEA: Prearrange to have one person stand in front of the group acting like a forlorn person needing support. Divide the rest of the participants into five small groups and assign each a proverb from question 6. Give the groups five minutes to develop a plan of action to support the forlorn person, utilizing principles from their proverb. Ask a representative from each group to come to the front and act out his or her supportive action.

Contributing with Comfort and Encouragement

KEY CONCEPT: Godly friendships are a source of encouragement.
GOAL: To use strengths acquired during trials to comfort others.

Traffic-lined streets, tension-filled jobs, and constantly rising prices can produce emotional stress. When people take out their frustrations on one another, stress increases and relationships suffer.

You can use stressful situations to build better relationships by supporting others with comfort and encouragement. An understanding word, a listening ear, or a helping hand can lift a person in a time of need. Contributing to others like this builds deeper relationships and causes the light of Christ's love to shine brightly.

1. "How can we experience joy even in a trying time like a loved one's death?"

2. "How does knowing that you are being equipped by God to help others make you feel about adversity?"

3. "Do you see any danger in overemphasizing the Second Coming? If so, why? If not, why not?"

4c. "People tend to think pastors and Christian leaders do not need encouragement or that they are too insignificant to encourage them. What are some ways we can encourage our pastor?"

5. "What kind of a friend do you want when you need business advice?"

   "When you are frustrated?"

   "When everything is going wrong?"

   "When you're overworked?"

   "What kind of a friend are you?"

6. "David does not mention any friends. How could he have benefited from others?"

   "Do you think that those around him were aware of his distress? What should you do when you become aware that someone is distressed?"

8. "How can we arrange to hold each other accountable to fulfill our projects?"

9. Incorporate the ideas from this question into a time of prayer for people you know who need comfort.

TEACHING IDEA: Illustrate three stages of adversity and comfort by drawing the pictures below on a large chart. Stage 1—Adversity comes into your life. Ask the group what you should do when this happens. (Draw on information outside this lesson.) Stage 2—Comfort comes from God. Get ideas from the group on the different forms this comfort may take—peace, adversity taken away, a problem turning into a blessing, etc. Stage 3—You comfort others who are in a similar situation. Get further ideas from class members on the way this can happen.

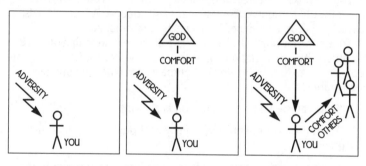

Divide the group into pairs (but not spouse with spouse). Ask one person in each pair to take thirty seconds to say encouraging things to the other. Then reverse roles for thirty seconds. Then let the entire group tell what they learned from the exercise.

Contributing to Spiritual Growth

KEY CONCEPT: You can enable people to grow spiritually by helping
   them learn and apply God's Word.
GOAL: To pray for others, feed them the Word, and live an exemplary life.

Pastors are not the only ministers. The Bible says every believer is a minister and can help others mature in Jesus Christ.

Your contribution to others will be progressive. Young Christians
can contribute through encouragement and support. As they grow spiritually, they become equipped to help people in other areas.

Your contribution will also correlate to the relationship you have
with others. An open relationship yields more opportunities for helping
people grow. As they grow, greater intimacy is reached, giving new
opportunities.

1. "How can we know that a person is growing spiritually?"

   "What does your definition imply you should do to help others
   grow?"

2. "How can you demonstrate Paul's depth of commitment to the
   people you minister to?"

   "What obstacles might we face when trying to contribute to
   others?"

   "What kinds of actions do you think this desire led Paul to do?"

   "What kinds of actions today would reflect the same desire?"

3. "Paul had this confidence for a church—can we have the same
   confidence for an individual? Why, or why not? How?"

4. "What are other ways to encourage and build up people?"

   "At the last session, we discussed your spiritual gifts. In what ways
   can you use your spiritual gifts to help others grow?"

5. "How is your ministry hindered if you do not have confidence?"

   "How is it hindered if you are self-confident?"

6. "Are the people to whom we minister always going to feel we love
   them? If not, should we change something?"

8. "Why is this action effective?" Ask for each action.

   "Which action utilizes your gifts most effectively?"

10. "Does Paul's command apply to you? Explain why or why not."

TEACHING IDEA: Divide the group into five small groups and assign each a different verse from question 8. Give them five minutes to brainstorm on practical ways to do the action suggested in the verse. Ask one person from each group to give a brief report to the entire group.

CONTRIBUTING 7
Viewing Discipline as a Contribution

KEY CONCEPT: God's loving discipline is our model.
GOAL: To welcome discipline because it is for your benefit.

A gruff sergeant, hands on hips, verbally assaulting a young soldier for a miscue while marching is not a good example of discipline. Neither is an irate boss, a frustrated parent, or an overbearing teacher. Yet, most people know little other than these models for what has often been called "discipline."

God is the ultimate example of discipline properly executed. Because we as humans fail so often to exercise discipline correctly, focusing on Him will help us understand how it contributes to others.

The proper use of discipline helps people reach their full potential. Perhaps the greatest reason people do not give corrective feedback to others is because they think no one wants to change. This negative attitude is wrong because it anticipates a wrong response.

1. "Why do you think tough love is essential to help people grow spiritually?"

    "A little three-year-old girl tripped while running, and a small piece of candy she had in her mouth lodged in her throat, choking her. A man seeing this quickly picked her up and gave her a sharp pat on the back, dislodging the candy. What do you think the girl thought about the man?"

    "How is she like us?"

    "How is the man like God?"

3. "Can we gain these benefits without being chastened? Explain."

4. "What do you think would happen to your life if God took away His discipline?"

5. "What will help us be Christlike in discipline? Be specific."

6. "What are the purposes of discipline? Of punishment?"

    "What are the motives and the actions of discipline?"

7. Here are some additional Scripture passages to consider: Psalm 94:12-14, Luke 12:47-48, John 15:1-8, 1 Corinthians 10:6-13, Hebrews 12:4-13.

8. "What are the dangers of ignoring discipline?"

    "What are the benefits of heeding discipline?"

"What is the ignorer like?"

"What is the heeder like?"

9. "What guidelines would you suggest for rebuke?"

"What attitude do we need to use discipline as a contribution?"

TEACHING IDEA: Bring a piece of bent wire or metal to illustrate truths from questions 1, 2, and 3. The wire represents a person who needs correction. Straightening it will make it more useful and improve its value, just like correction will help our lives. If the metal is pliable, it can be straightened with little or no problem. If it is not pliable, you would need to heat it in order to straighten it. In the same way, God may need to apply the heat of adversity to our lives to make us pliable for His correction. The heat is not motivated by anger, but by a desire to improve our value and make us more useful.

Contributing by Discipline

KEY CONCEPT: Discipline is for improvement, not to vent anger.
GOAL: To use discipline for others' benefit and to build close relationships.

Although discipline always involves correction, it does not need to be
harsh. An understanding word and gentle suggestion often help a person
see what to change and how to do it. Correction, combined with encouragement like this, is discipline at its best.

Discipline is based on close relationships and can produce even more
intimate ones. If it is used to "put someone in his place," it won't build
closeness. And it is not likely to make a contribution.

Discipline is a potent spice. The church properly seasoned with it has
a good flavor. Too much can be overpowering and ruin the recipe.

1. "What made this experience so positive?"

   "What has been your relationship with the person who disciplined
   you?"

2. "Under what circumstances should you rebuke an unwise person?"

3. "What qualification, according to this verse, do we need in order to
   rebuke?"

   "What does it mean to be 'spiritual'?"

4. "What should you do if you don't think a person rebuking you has
   these attitudes?"

   "When rebuking another, what are some good ways to communicate these attitudes?"

5. "What does the analogy in the verse mean to you?"

   "What is unwise rebuke?"

6a. "What kind of person would require a Timothy-style rebuke?"

6b. "What kind of person would require a Titus-style rebuke?"

   "What will help us use both styles?"

8. "What will help us be more consistent in the correct use of rebuke
   and discipline?"

9. "Do you think this passage applies if someone has hurt your feelings by not saying 'Hello'?"

   "What is the purpose of these steps?"

TEACHING IDEA: Illustrate Matthew 18:15-20 with the diagram below. Draw in the train and the primary goal of better relationships. The first track to accomplish the goal would be the straight line of "private talk." Only when this does not work (draw a barrier to this line) should you begin on the next track (add track and words "Go with two or three" to the goal of establishing words). If this doesn't work (add next barrier), we try another track (add next line and goal). If this doesn't work, we have our final line of action. After presenting this, be sure to reemphasize the fact that the secondary tracks are added only when barriers are erected.

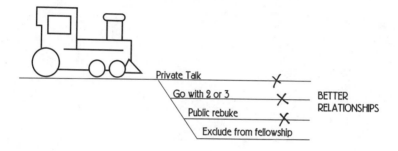

COMMUNICATING

COMMUNICATING **1**
Speaking Appropriately

KEY CONCEPT: Communication reflects your inner state.
GOAL: To use clear communications that build relationships.

Using words is one of the main ways we communicate with one another. We speak words, we write words, and we think words.

We enhance words with gestures, motions, and expressions. We use undertones, overtones, and monotones. We add idioms, metaphors, and hyperbole.

All of our communication devices are important because relationships require communication. Improving communication opens doors to improved relationships.

1. The following exercise shows the value of both words and gestures. Ask for two pairs of volunteers. One person will use words but no gestures (without saying the key word) to get his or her partner to draw something. One person in the other pair will use gestures alone to get his or her partner to say something. The key word is "heart." One pair should leave the room until the first has completed the exercise.

2. "How do people violate these guidelines of effective communication?"

3. "Do some people purposely use these obstacles? Why? How?"

4. "Why do you think Jesus called these people 'a brood of vipers'? How were they like vipers?"

5. "In the same style as James, how would you complete the following?"

   "The tongue is like a gun because . . ."

   "The tongue is like a car because . . ."

   "The tongue is like rain because . . ."

7. "How can we generalize this 'replacement process' for other areas of our lives?"

   "Why is it better to replace wrong communication with good communication than to just stop it?"

8. "What practical steps help you 'be filled with the Spirit' or 'have the Word dwell in you'?"

9. "How can we reword this proverb into modern-day language?"

TEACHING IDEA: For question 4, use a drawing like the one below to illustrate the teaching of Matthew 12:33-37. The roots of the tree absorb elements from the ground. The same elements come out in the fruit of the tree. When people feed on sinful ideas, the fruit of their communication is evil. These things must be replaced with other things. (Erase "sins" and write in "graciousness," "kindness," "love," etc.)

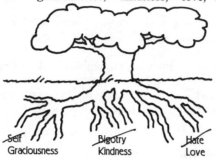

Self
Graciousness

Bigotry
Kindness

Hate
Love

Listening Attentively

KEY CONCEPT: Fast ears are better than a fast tongue.
GOAL: To listen to the words and also the feelings of others.

It is not unusual for a person who has just been introduced to another to say, "What was your name again?" Most of the time the problem was not partial deafness; it was inattentiveness.

If our minds are consumed with thoughts about ourselves and the way we impress others, there may not be space left to register the name of another. When we love others we focus on them and what they say. Listening is an important part of love.

1. "What are some common reasons people don't listen?"

2. "Give a real-life example of each proverb."

   "Have you ever been introduced to someone and two minutes later couldn't recall his or her name? Why did this happen? What was your mind doing when it should have been listening?"

3. "It is easy to say 'apply the wisdom you hear,' but what exactly does that mean?"

4. "How many people in our group have ever said, 'You don't listen to me'? When you said that, what feelings were you attempting to communicate? Were you angry? Why?"

5. "What attitudes did the Thessalonians have that we should also have?"

6. "Did Jesus address this to the listener or to someone who was intervening between the speaker and listener?"

7. "How many different ways can you think of listening?"

   "Which way does Jesus want us to listen?"

8. "What should you do if you suddenly realize you haven't heard the last two or three sentences in a conversation?"

TEACHING IDEA: As you begin the meeting have someone put a distraction in front of the group. The distraction may be a pet in a cage, a person wearing a mask, or someone sitting quietly but looking all around. Then read a couple of paragraphs from a story.

Next ask some questions to determine who listened attentively to you read and who were too distracted. Since there are so many distractions in life, this shows that listening requires discipline and energy. Ask the group what things distract them from listening attentively.

Acting Consistently

KEY CONCEPT: Your actions are regarded more than your words.
GOAL: To consistently act in a loving manner.

People find it difficult to believe what a person says when that person's actions don't back it up. It is easy to say you care, but it takes effort to do caring things.

This effort transforms intention into action. Many people think they have communicated their care when they say, with deep sincerity, "That poor person. I want to do something to help." But the best intentions have often failed.

1. "A person who is hard of hearing may speak so loudly that it seems to you he is angry. What are other ways people easily misinterpret actions?"

2a. "What do you think is the best evidence of a relationship with Jesus Christ?"

   "What actions that Jesus did not command do many expect from Christians?"

3. The word *hypocrite* is often misapplied to people who have imperfections or inconsistencies. It means someone who is *pretending* to be something he or she is not.

   "Don't we all, at times, pretend to be something we are not?"

4. "This was spoken about a church. What do you think would cause our community to talk about us in a positive way?"

5. "Why did the Jews not accept Samaritans?"

   "How is that like people today?"

   "Did Jesus accept everyone? Explain."

6a. Divide into pairs. A asks B, "What is love?" B answers without using an expression given in the passage. Then B asks A the same thing. Repeat for at least five cycles.

7. "Did Jesus ever do something that caused people to wonder if He loved them? What? Why?"

8a. "The Samaritan spent his time, his money, and his emotions in helping the man. Which of these is most difficult for you to spend? Why?"

"What should you do to make it easier for you to do this?"

9. "How can the way we dress help communicate acceptance? The recreation we have? The decor of our homes?"

10. "Would our church be better if we had more minorities attending?"

TEACHING IDEA: Conduct a skit where your words and actions are inconsistent. For example, ask a husband and wife to act very indifferent and cold while saying things like, "I love you," "I'm glad I married you." After the skit, ask the group which they would believe, the words or the actions.

Tell the group that smaller groups will be formed for question 6. Each group will discuss one action that shows love from 1 Corinthians 13:4-7. Allow the people to choose the action they desire to discuss. Once the groups are established, have them discuss these questions: (1) Why is this action important to you? (2) How do you feel when people act this way toward you? (3) What are the biggest hindrances to acting this way?

The exercise in 6 also works well in a classroom setting.

Communicating Wisely

KEY CONCEPT: Righteousness results in wise communication.
GOAL: To speak wisely, appropriately, and thoughtfully.

This lesson is a study of communication from the book of Proverbs—a book of wisdom. More teaching about communication occurs in this book of the Bible than any other.

The wisdom of Proverbs is practical—it tells you how to behave wisely. It is profound—there are deep issues to understand. It is time-less—the same truths that applied to Solomon 3,000 years ago apply today.

1. "How do you react when you hear clear but unwise communication?"

   "How do you react when you hear wise but poorly communicated speech?"

2. "What are some fragile things highly subject to destruction by words?"

   "Is there a time when it is wise not to be soft-spoken? Explain."

4. Start the discussion by telling one reason you need to be more soft-spoken. Encourage others in the group to do the same.

   "Does increasing the volume of your voice improve others' understanding? What does?"

5. "What examples of these results have you seen?"

6. "If a person who rarely utters a word is a 'one' and a chatterbox is a 'ten,' give the number that best describe the kind of person you find it easiest to build a relationship with? Why?"

   "In what circumstances do you tend to speak when you should be silent?"

   "In what circumstances do you tend to be silent when you should speak out?"

7. "What else can happen in a church when favoritism takes place?"

8. "How do you benefit when speaking wisely?"

   "How do others benefit?"

10. "What are some examples of these results?"

TEACHING IDEA: Put the addition problems illustrated below on a large chart without the answers at the bottom. Explain you are studying Proverbs and how to speak wisely. Ask group members to look up the references and draw conclusions to put down as the "sum" of the addition problems.

11:9-11	15:1	10:19
18:21	15:4	13:3
+21:23	+25:15	+17:27-28
=	=	=

Bring the following items to the session and show them while teaching the proverbs in question 9: some gold jewelry for 25:12; a fan (representing the cooling of snow) for 25:13; a glass of ice water for 25:25; some lotion for 27:9.

Communicating Unwisely

KEY CONCEPT: Foolish talk harms you and others.
GOAL: To replace harmful speech with wise utterances.

To communicate wisely as learned in the previous lesson, foolish, harmful, and senseless speech need to be eliminated. Ephesians 4:29 directs us to replace unwholesome talk with thanksgiving. In the same way, all unwise communication should be replaced with wise communication. Silence may stop foolish speech, but it does not provide the benefits of wise speech.

1. "Do you think a salesperson would make more or fewer sales by following the guidelines of wise speech from the previous lesson?"

2. "How is their speech like a 'gusher'?"

   "How is it like a fire?"

   "For whom do they talk about trouble?"

3. "What are some of the reasons people gossip?"

   "Why is gossip so harmful?"

   "Why is it so unwise (that is, how does it hurt the one who gossips)?"

4. "What often happens when you talk to the subject of gossip?"

6a. "What do you do to 'let another praise you'?"

7. "When is humor foolish?"

   "Is the capacity to repeat great quantities of factual information knowledge? Wisdom? Foolishness? What?"

8. "It appears that these two directives oppose one another. Should you do one some of the time and the other at other times? Should we find some balance between these two?"

10. "Why do people use barbed or insulting humor?"

11. "Hebrews 4:15 says Jesus was tempted in every way like we are. What kind of foolish speech do you think Jesus was tempted to use?"

TEACHING IDEA: Put the following numbered statements on separate slips of paper and hand them to people.

1. Getting drunk is good for you because it rids you of inhibitions.

2. If I ever need money, I'll rob a bank.

3. Did everyone hear about my neighbor running off with the mail carrier?

4. I think your ideas are the greatest; you can do everything so well, and you're too beautiful for words.

5. I'm really one of the best in my profession—no, I guess I am the best.

6. The most important issue facing our church today is the continuation of the mutual support for the bilateral agreement of the second-degree ecumenical accord on orthodox ecclesiology.

Prepare other slips with these references from Proverbs and give them to others: Proverbs 15:14, 15:28, 18:6-7, 18:8, 20:6, 20:19, 24:1-2, 27:2.

Make duplicates if necessary, so you can distribute one slip of paper (either a statement or reference) to each person. Then play a game where each person with a reference must find a person with a statement that corresponds to it. (There is more than one corresponding statement for some references.) After everyone has found a statement, ask each person to read the statement and the proverb.

Communicating Honestly with Yourself

KEY CONCEPT: Confidence in God's mercy helps you be honest.
GOAL: To freely admit to yourself and to God what you are—good and
bad.

The witness gave his story with a steady voice and clear eyes. No one
doubted his sincerity. A lie detector confirmed that there were no sub-
conscious reactions indicating a falsehood. His reputation for telling the
truth spanned years. Yet, the rest of the evidence undeniably showed he
had lied.

He didn't think he was lying. He told the story as best he remem-
bered the facts. But it was horrendously in error because he had failed to
be honest with himself. And now he no longer knew the truth, he knew
only what he told himself.

1. "How can we be honest with ourselves and still preserve our
   dignity?"

2. "What is one way you are somewhat like this person?"

3. "Does God intend for us to feel bad about ourselves? If not, how
   can we honestly face our enormous inconsistencies and still not
   feel bad about ourselves?"

4. "What general principles can we conclude from these lists of
   characteristics?"

   "When is it most difficult for you to be honest about yourself?"

5. "If we know we are all sinners, why do many still have such a hard
   time admitting it?"

7. "Do you think Paul was giving up?"

   "Was Paul failing to take responsibility for his life? Explain."

8. "What helps you keep your trust in God?"

   "Is it possible to think you are trusting God while really trusting in
   self? Explain."

10. "If honesty was graded on a scale with 1 being totally dishonest and
    100 being totally honest, and if your self-honesty grade is 70, what
    do you think would be your honesty grade with others?"

11. "Do we need practical steps to be self-honest, or is it just a case of
    doing it? If we need steps, what are they? If not, what are our obsta-
    cles to self-honesty?"

TEACHING IDEA: Divide the participants into small groups. Ask half of the groups to use Psalm 51 to devise a profile of a person who is honest with himself. Ask the other half to use Psalm 52:1-5 to profile a person who is dishonest with himself. Give seven minutes for this exercise and three minutes for each group to report.

Communicating Honestly with Others

KEY CONCEPT: Honesty in tense situations often requires wisdom and
   tact.
GOAL: To express love and honesty at the same time.

Your boss asks you how you like his latest idea. You do not care for it, but
it is obvious he wants you to say you like his idea. If you express anything
less than full approval, it is likely he will argue the issue with you until
you do agree. Since he is persuasive and you are not, you want to avoid
debate. "Now is not the time," you say to yourself—but what do you say
to him?

   Some tense situations can be handled with a verbal parry. "My! What
a baby!" often appeases a proud parent. At other times the issues are
paramount and directness is required.

1. "Do you actually think honesty is the best policy in the situation
   you described?"

   "Can you think of any present-day situations where a person might
   be tempted to lie for what might seem to be a worthy purpose?"

2. "Although no scripture indicates that God ranks some sins as more
   vile than others, how evil do you think it is to lie?"

3. "How do 'white lies' affect your relationships?"

4. "What happens when you speak truth without love or love without
   truth?"

5. "How do you feel when you get a negative response to your
   honesty?"

6. "Did everyone think Jesus was a loving person? Explain."

   "Do you think Jesus would have encountered less animosity from
   certain people if He had used more diplomacy? If no, why? If yes,
   why didn't He use more?"

7. Divide into two teams and ask each team to devise a tense situation
   for the other team to respond to by speaking the truth in love. The
   situations should be realistic and likely to happen to people in the
   group.

8. "Were there other times when speaking the truth caused greater
   tension? What then should be our motivation for speaking the
   truth?"

9. "How can we protect ourselves?"

10. "What philosophies today are hurting many Christians? How?"

"How does television deceive many?"

12. "What have you learned in your study this week that is helping you defeat a deception?"

TEACHING IDEA: Arrange in advance for two people to act out the following two situations:

Narrator: "Susan is twenty-four years old and lives alone in an apartment. She works as a teacher in public schools. She has spent her money on expensive or 'unneeded' clothes, eating in restaurants, and other unnecessary luxuries. She is now broke, and the rent is due tomorrow. She has just explained this to her father."

In the first drama the father should rebuke the daughter, be firm, offer to help her with a budget, etc., but not give her the money.

In the second drama, the father should be totally warm and responsive—offering the money and his help at any time.

After the two dramas, ask the group to discuss good and bad points of each as they apply to speaking the truth in love.

Communicating the Good News

KEY CONCEPT: Failing to communicate the gospel is like withholding water from a thirsty person.

GOAL: To prepare ourselves to communicate the good news to those in our society.

Imagine that Jonas Salk, after discovering the beneficial qualities of penicillin, decided not to tell anyone about it. You might consider him a murderer or a monster. Certainly he would have been less than loving.

The healing capacity of penicillin is minute compared to that of the gospel of Jesus Christ. It touches only the body; the gospel affects our spirit, our soul, our emotions, our relationships, and our eternal destiny. Our responsibility and privilege is communicating the gospel to our society.

1. "Did the uniqueness of the communication enhance your joy of the good news you received?"

2. "Imagine for a moment that there is no life after death. What reasons would there still be to communicate the gospel?"

   "Do the majority of people in our society want answers to life or to gaining life after death?"

   "How can we prepare ourselves to communicate the gospel to the majority?"

3. "What is an example of seasoning your speech with salt?"

4. "How should these questions be answered?"

   "What are some smoke-screen questions?"

   "Should they be answered? If so, how?"

5. "A man retrieved a money bag dropped by an armored vehicle and returned it. Many people said they thought he was foolish. Are people today attracted by good works, as they were in biblical times? What kinds of good works do attract people?"

7. "If we tell people these facts, have we communicated the good news? If not, what part of the gospel is good news to them?"

   "What have you found to be effective in communicating the good news of the gospel?"

8. "Describe the kind of person you are most likely to talk to who is ready to hear the gospel. What is an effective way to communicate with that person?"

9. "How have people responded when you told them of your spiritual journey?"

TEACHING IDEA: Choose a situation that people in the group are likely to encounter and role-play communicating the gospel to someone. If the person to whom you are talking is a neighbor or another continuing contact, prepare three short acts following the outline below.

Act 1—Conversation over coffee. You tell how much fun you had at a Sunday school party. Your friend says something about thinking about going to Sunday school again. You invite your friend.

Act 2—After attending a class, your friend asks a question about what was taught. You answer the question and go on to say some things about the gospel.

Act 3—Conversation over coffee again. You ask your friend, "Have you thought any more about . . . ?" Your friend responds positively, so you continue to explain the gospel more completely.

Opening Doors for the Good News

KEY CONCEPT: Good relationships, like plowed soil, provide a receptive environment for communicating the gospel.

GOAL: To cultivate relationships with nonChristians that lead to opportunities to discuss spiritual matters.

Our responsibility in communicating the good news goes beyond delivering the message. We should cultivate the soil by building a friendship. In some cases the door opens almost immediately. Other times there will be dozens of conversations before a person is ready to listen and honestly consider the claims of the gospel.

Those who do not take time to build a degree of friendship often treat people as targets to hit with their verbal bullets. Not surprisingly, the targets erect shields to ward off the communique.

1. "No door should ever be considered permanently closed. What should we do to open some of these closed doors?"

2. Dividing a prayer project into smaller steps can provide encouragement to continue to pray as the steps are fulfilled. In one case prayer for a drug-addicted nephew in a distant city had these steps: meet a Christian, establish a relationship with the Christian, attend some spiritual meetings, talk about problems with the Christian, listen to the gospel, say yes to Christ.

3. "How can we check to see if we have an open door with a person?"

   "What are some questions or statements you have found helpful in beginning a conversation on spiritual matters?"

4. "Is there any situation in which we should not use an open door with an individual? If so, when?"

6. "Let's brainstorm and see how many different team positions for communicating the gospel we can think of."

7. "The eunuch invited Philip to explain the Scriptures to him. What experiences have you had with wide-open doors like this? What should be done in these situations?"

8c. "The Athenians were interested in spiritual matters but did not seem particularly positive about Jesus Christ or the Scriptures. What experiences have you had with similar situations? What should be done in these cases?"

9. "What kinds of people have been most responsive to our church? To our group? To us as individuals?"

TEACHING IDEA: Bring two small pots for plants to class. In one put some poor soil and casually toss a seed on top. In the other put some potting soil, plant a seed properly, and water it. Then ask, "Which of these two pots is mostly likely to produce the fruit desired?" The seed represents the message. The preparation of the pots represents our relationships.

DEVELOPING UNITY

DEVELOPING UNITY 1
Two Become One

KEY CONCEPT: In marriage, two people become one.
GOAL: To express the unity of marriage with fidelity and faithfulness.

In marriage, two people are one by God's decree. Although this unity is established by God, it does not guarantee that married people will always act in harmony. Following the teachings on loving one another enables couples to live as one. God's Spirit provides the power for each person to behave properly in the marriage relationship.

Married couples reflect Jesus Christ in His relationship to the Church when they live in the unity described in the Bible. They are a picture of God's love and the Body's response.

1. "What ideas do you have for a wedding that would represent two becoming one?"

2. "What do you think most people want out of marriage?"

   "Which of these expectations are legitimate?"

3. "Why do the purposes we listed in question 2 need the unity we described in question 3?"

4. "This passage refers to two uses of sex, a good one and a bad one. What are the penalties (or results) of wrong uses of sex?"

   "What are the benefits of the right use of sex?"

5. "What problems can ensue if there is emotional involvement with someone other than your spouse?"

6. "How should married people deal with adultery?"

   "What practical steps can a person take to avoid committing adultery?"

7. "What helps you and your spouse to become best friends?"

   "How can you attain unity of thought, emotions, values, etc.?"

8,9. "Why has divorce become more prevalent among church members?"

   "How can we express love and acceptance toward those who have a divorce in their past and maintain a scriptural attitude toward divorce?"

10. Ask each married couple to stand and hold hands while they read the selected passage.

TEACHING IDEA: Bring two flashlights and two different colors of cellophane to the meeting. Put the cellophane over the lens of each flashlight. Shine the two flashlights on the wall. Then focus both beams on one spot. The two lights merge and become one beam of light, illustrating two becoming one in marriage. Other ways this demonstration illustrates marriage are the greater intensity of the combined beam and the fact that the individual colors of the two flashlights are lost as they merge to become a new color.

DEVELOPING UNITY **2**
Functioning as One

KEY CONCEPT: Husbands and wives are equally important in a
marriage.
GOAL: To fulfill personal responsibility without evaluating the performance of one's spouse.

The power train of an automobile illustrates the working together of husband and wife in marriage. The motor and transmission are very dissimilar, with different functions. One is not more important than the other; the car doesn't run without both operating properly. In addition, the car won't move if both are in good operating condition but not linked together correctly.

So, in marriage, things run smoothly when both husband and wife are properly united and fulfilling their roles.

1. "In what ways is this activity different from marriage?"

2. "What are the most important areas for agreement?"

   "Is it possible that the areas of agreement are too inconsequential to 'walk together'? What do you do then?"

3. "What implications can you draw from these lists?"

4c. Additional references you may wish to consult are: Matthew 7:1, Romans 2:1, 1 Corinthians 4:5.

5. Ask the married people in your group to think of a time when they felt they suffered unjustly in their marriage. Then, without responding aloud, have them ask themselves these questions:

   ▶ "Did your partner intend for you to suffer?"
   ▶ "What did you actually suffer?"
   ▶ "Have you ever caused your partner to suffer in a similar way?"

   Then ask the married people to share any insights they gained from this exercise.

6. "How would you describe a virtuous man?"

8. "Is marriage fair? Should it be? Explain."

TEACHING IDEA: Bring a hand-cranked egg-beater to the meeting. Hold it up and crank it saying, "This is a marriage functioning as one." Then put a spoon or other obstacle between the beaters so it won't work. Hold it up, try to crank it, and say, "This is marriage where the two parties function independently."

DEVELOPING UNITY **3**
Family Foundations

KEY CONCEPT: The family is the primary unit of society.
GOAL: To order priorities so family relationships receive proper attention.

The high priority God places on the family is seen throughout Scripture. The family was the first social group established in history. Old Testament governments were organized by family units. Jesus made provision for His mother while hanging on the cross. There are over 10,000 references in the Bible to family relationships.

In our highly mobile society an increasing number of people live great distances from family members. A deep and lasting foundation of relationships needs to be established to benefit from the support only family can provide.

1. Ask each group member to tell briefly about his or her family including number of siblings, where they grew up, what home was like, etc.

2. "What are some of the implications of the importance of the family?"

3. "What are some things we can do to help our children have good memories of our families?"

4. "If you were to devise another command, what would it be?"

   "To whom would it be given? Why?"

5. "For what was the family important in Bible times?"

   "For what is the family important in our culture?"

   "What advantages have we gained?"

   "What advantages have we lost?"

6. "Which church programs help accomplish this goal?"

   "Are there church programs that hinder the quality of family relationships? Explain."

8. "What should you do if the person is your parent? Your sibling? Your grandparent? Your child?

   "What should you do if you feel there are unresolved issues with a family member who has died?"

   "Although nothing can guarantee a positive relationship, once you have established a good relationship with a family member, is there anything additional you can do? What?"

TEACHING IDEA: Ask four volunteers to stand in a circle in front of the group (to represent father, mother, and two children). Identify each in the following way: father—a big old T-shirt with holes; mother—a floppy hat with flowers; first child—a set of bicycle handlebars (or wheel from bicycle); second child—a baby's rattle.

Ask someone else to read Colossians 3:18-21, stopping every time a responsibility is given. Then stretch a piece of string between the two people involved in the responsibility. Drape a folded piece of paper over the string with the command written on the paper. This exercise will illustrate the relationships and various responsibilities in a family.

DEVELOPING UNITY 4
Family Responsibilities

KEY CONCEPT: Parents form the basic values of the family.
GOAL: For children to be pliable as parents mold them into godly adults.

There probably have never been parents who held a class for their children on "How to Be Disobedient," or "How to Be Judgmental," or "The Advantages of Cheating." Parents generally try to communicate the exact opposite of these things. But many have become a primary source of teaching these characteristics by practicing them, by withholding correction, and by failing to teach better virtues.

Parents have the responsibility to be good molders of their children. Children have the responsibility to be flexible clay. Rebellion and disobedience are lumps that cause distortions and ugliness.

Submission and cooperation remove these lumps and allow true beauty to result—the beauty that results from the unity of the family being exercised.

1a. "Did you learn any important lessons from handling this responsibility?"

2. "What helps us fulfill these responsibilities?"

3. "What are some of the most effective ways of teaching your children?"

   "Who are your allies in teaching?"

   "Who are your enemies in teaching?"

4. "What happens when anger enters the discipline process?"

   "What should parents do if they feel they need to 'vent their emotions'?"

   "How can we know when to be firm and when to be merciful?"

5. "What part of your church experience is helping you accomplish your goals?"

6. "What is something adults can do to reflect these ideas in their relationship to their parents?"

   "How do some adults create unnecessary obstacles to children being able to fulfill their responsibilities?"

7. "The Recabites accepted extra responsibilities as a way of life. What extra responsibilities can we accept that would help our parents? Our children? Our family? Our church?"

8. "How can the characteristics of family relationships be applied in our church family?"

"Can we maintain these relationships with everyone in our church? If not, with whom should we maintain these relationships?"

TEACHING IDEA: Across the top of the chalkboard make a list of the topics on which parental teaching should center from question 3. Then under this list make three columns titled "Enemies," "Neutral," and "Allies." There is a battle for the minds, values, and morals of children. Our job is to establish the correct values and morals as brought out in these passages.

Then read the following list one at a time and ask the group members to indicate the appropriate column for each: school, television, church, movies, dinner table, rock music, dances, roller-skating, picnics, etc. Add a few of your own. When you finish reading your list, ask the participants if they have any additions to the three columns.

Dynamic Fellowship

KEY CONCEPT: Unity in the local church is demonstrated by love, care, and support.

GOAL: To participate in a local fellowship that helps you be the person God intends.

The Bible presents the local church as people in right relationship with God and with one another. According to Scripture, the church is not a building, denomination, or program. Unity in a church leads people to worship, serve, care, and have a colorful witness to the rest of the world.

When a local church does not function in unity, worship stagnates, their service becomes legalistic, and their witness lackluster. When people follow the biblical patterns, they recapture dynamic fellowship, deep relationships, and continuing unity.

1. "Which activities in our church help you the most to grow spiritually?"

2. Read all of Psalm 133. "David went on to say that unity is like precious oil and like dew. To what else can unity be likened?"

3. "Is it possible for people to seem to be fellowshiping when they really are not? Explain."

4. "Are there other things you consider important to healthy fellowship?"

   "How does transparency help fellowship?"

   "What causes some people to insist on doctrinal agreement?"

5a. "What should we do to help some of these suggestions become reality?"

6. "What happens to a group of people when they are experiencing these activities?"

8c. "What do you think are the long-range effects of people attending church meetings that do not foster these results?"

10. "Should a church that is not growing numerically focus attention on outreach or more dynamic fellowship? Explain."

TEACHING IDEA: Divide the group into smaller groups. Ask each group to do the exercise in question 5. Afterward, ask a representative from each group to give a report on the most encouraging thing about your church and the best suggestion for adding more love, care, and support.

Divide the group into pairs. Give the first person in each pair one minute to pay compliments to the other. Then reverse the roles. Afterward, give several in the group an opportunity to tell how this helps build unity in the fellowship.

Deepening Relationships

KEY CONCEPT: Christ has opened the door to greater intimacy with other believers.

GOAL: To cultivate a core of intimate friends from among those with whom you fellowship.

A pastor listened as the speaker challenged his audience: "Whom would you call if you were considering suicide and could call only one person?" Later, in tears, the pastor told the speaker he couldn't think of anyone to call.

Having strong biblical relationships with others is a wonderful benefit, but there are situations when we desire more. We desire an intimate, deep friendship like David had with Jonathan or Paul with Timothy. Paul said, "I have no one else like him. . . . As a son with his father he has served with me" (Philippians 2:20-22).

1. "What seem to be some of the main factors in deepening relationships?"

   "Which experiences that you listed were intentional?"

2. Ask each participant to give one example of the qualities he or she listed.

3. "Do your answers indicate that there is a problem in the church?"

   "What is the problem?"

   "What responsibility do you have to resolve it?"

   "Would courage help you be honest?"

   "What can you do to overcome hindrances to being honest?"

4. "What sins do you think James 5:16 is telling us to confess?"

   "To whom should we confess?"

5. "What needs did Paul indirectly indicate?"

6. "What other principles of developing relationships have you learned from the LOVE ONE ANOTHER series?"

   "What other references do you think answer this question?"

7. "Why do so few men today have the kind of relationship David and Jonathan had?"

   "What can be done to correct this?"

8. "One practical way of improving relationships with others is to have breakfast or lunch together. What other suggestions do you have?"

TEACHING IDEA: Hold up a sheet of typing paper and tell the group it represents a good relationship. The whiteness represents love and concern. The smooth edge represents smoothness in communication. You can also write statements or scriptures about good relationships. Yet the relationship still is somewhat fragile and subject to being rent. Demonstrate by tearing the paper in two. Now start with a new piece of paper and when you talk about a deepening activity, fold the paper in half lengthwise. Repeat, always folding lengthwise. You should be able to fold the paper four or five times. Now ask someone to attempt to tear the paper in half. A deeper relationship will withstand a great deal of stress.

Unity of Believers

KEY CONCEPT: We are all one in Christ.

GOAL: To accept and appreciate every believer as a brother or sister in Christ.

1. "What culture(s) would you not want to minister to? Why not?"

   "In all probability all of us are uncomfortable in some churches. Is that wrong? Are we prejudiced?"

2. "It is clear that people believe different things. So, what does 'one faith' mean?"

3. "What helps maintain the unity of the Spirit?"

   "Does this mean we should not discuss different ideas and values?"

4a. "How are the Jew-Gentile problem of the first century and racial problems of today similar?"

5. "Do you think Jesus' prayer is being answered? If so, account for the tension we see between some Christians. If not, why not?"

6. "How can we convert some of these possibilities into realities?"

7. "Which action and/or attitude do you consider to be most important in promoting unity?"

   "Which is most influential in causing disunity?"

8. "In what ways have you begun to exercise unity with believers since studying these topics?"

9. Consider the possibility of hosting a group from a church with different ethnic, cultural, or doctrinal differences.

TEACHING IDEA: Write the words "Jew" and "Gentile" on a large chart with a wide barrier between them. Write in one or two barriers. Ask the group what other things can contribute to the barrier. Ask someone to read Ephesians 2:11-19. Whenever the passage says some part of the barrier is eliminated in Christ, cross this part off. In the end, use the general statement from verse 14 to show the entire barrier is eliminated in Christ.

JEW		GENTILE
	Prejudice	
	Superiority and inferiority feelings	
	Religious differences	
	Other problems	

When finished, cross off "Jew" and "Gentile" and write in "Blacks" and "Whites," or another racial difference, and show that the same principles are true for this situation also.

Universal Human Dignity

KEY CONCEPT: All people have dignity from being made in God's image.
GOAL: To respect and honor every person as a reflection of God.

God created every person in His image. Each one has potential to glorify Him. God's mark on every person links all people together in unity. Appreciating the unity of this godlikeness enables people to see the worth, dignity, and value of every person.

Because people have such value, it is worth the time and effort it takes to develop relationships with others. When Christians develop friendships with nonChristians based on the dignity of humanity, nonbelievers become more than mere targets for evangelistic thrusts. This does not mean that evangelism will not take place. But the gospel will be shared with people in a way that recognizes their value.

1. "Which, if any, show that humans are better than the rest of creation?"

2. "Which aspects of dignity do you create for yourself?"

   "Which, if any, do you get from others?"

3. There are many similarities between God and humans, such as the ability to communicate, have feelings, have intellect, be creative, etc. These similarities do not define fully what is meant by bearing God's image, but they help us understand some aspects of it.

4. "What is the logic of not cursing people when so many things they do are so perverse?"

5. "What can be done about deep-seated prejudices created by our environment and society?"

6. "What significance do you see to these things?"

7. "What are some additional common characteristics?"

9. "What do you think would happen if people fully realized the dignity God has given them by creating them in His image?"

TEACHING IDEA: For question 3, prepare a number of index cards with short general statements about God on each one. Include statements like: "God creates," "God is moral," "God communicates," "God cares," "God is involved with people," "God has emotion," etc. If possible, prepare one card for each participant. (If the group is very large, use only ten to fifteen cards.) Ask each person to read his or her card and explain a similarity in human beings that shows we are like God and, therefore, have great dignity.

Universal Human Need

KEY CONCEPT: All people have sinned and need God's mercy.
GOAL: To be involved in helping others find God's mercy in Jesus
   Christ.

We all have been created in the image of God, and we all are the children
of Adam. Bearing God's image means we all have His mark on us. We
reproduce many of His characteristics. Like Him, we are creative, willful,
emotional, and capable of love.

   Adam, too, has left his mark on us. After he had sinned, he passed on
to all his offspring the sinful nature. It obscures the image of God in us
and causes us to perform sinful actions.

1. "What terms other than *sin* do people use to describe their imperfections?"

   "Why do many not like the term *sinners?*"

2. "Can you give an example of these steps in action?"

3. "Which activities listed in this passage are not wrong in themselves?"

   "When are they wrong?"

4. "What keeps other people from coming to this same conclusion?"

   "If we carried out this example to the extreme, we would never
   punish any lawbreaker. Where is the boundary? What is the
   balance?"

6. "What are some practical steps that help us to relate to nonChristians in this way?"

7a. "Do you think it is easier to obey these commands today or in biblical times? Why?"

8. "What are some guidelines that indicate when we are too separated
   from nonbelievers?"

   "What would indicate when we are too close to nonbelievers?"

9. "What is one example for each element of successful witnessing
   listed in this passage?"

10. "What made you thirsty to hear the gospel?"

   "What salty sayings help produce the same thirst in others?"

11. "What benefit would there be to inviting these people to your home? Church? A party?"

TEACHING IDEA: Draw a large meter on a chart displayed in front of the group, like the illustration below. Then ask people to read the references from questions 6, 8, and 9 and write the concepts that identify a relationship to nonChristians that is either too close, too remote, or just right.

RELATING TO NONCHRISTIANS

BALANCED
1. In, not of the world
2.
3.

TOO CLOSE
1. Partnership
2.
3.

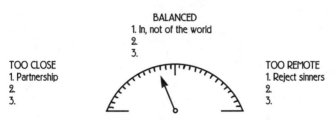

TOO REMOTE
1. Reject sinners
2.
3.

Churches Alive!

This study is just one item in a wide range of small group material authored by Churches Alive. Continue your study with other books in this series.

Churches Alive has local representatives who provide their own living expenses to serve you at your church. On-site support and training conferences will develop commitment and vision in group leaders. Our experienced staff can help you develop leaders, enrich your groups, and reach out to others.

Conferences and Support Services

A Pastor's Perspective:

"Churches Alive was a tremendous help to us when we were getting started in our discipleship ministry. We had to make a choice—either try to learn ourselves and make a lot of mistakes, or get some help and minimize mistakes. Their careful but goal-oriented approach helps any church build a solid, perpetuating ministry."

Churches Alive!
600 Meridian Avenue
Suite 200
San Jose, CA 95126
(408) 294-6000
(408) 294-6029 FAX

Conferences

Designed to strengthen the effectiveness of your leaders, our conferences and seminars range from one to four days. Most are taught by Churches Alive staff and local pastors. In addition, we arrange special seminars in your church to encourage people in your church to study the Bible.

Support Services

In dozens of denominations, our staff helps churches large and small. We can help you evaluate, plan, train leaders, and expand your small groups. Invite a Churches Alive representative to explore small group discipleship at your church.

Call 1-800-755-3787